Forecasting in Foodservice

Forecasting in Foodservice

ANN M. MESSERSMITH
Oregon State University

JUDY L. MILLER
Kansas State University

John Wiley & Sons, Inc.
New York • Chichester • Brisbane • Toronto • Singapore

In recognition of the importance of preserving what has been
written, it is a policy of John Wiley & Sons, Inc., to have
books of enduring value published in the United States
printed on acid-free paper, and we exert our best efforts
to that end.

Copyright © 1992 by John Wiley & Sons, Inc.

All rights reserved. Published simultaneously in Canada.

Reproduction or translation of any part of this work
beyond that permitted by Section 107 or 108 of the
1976 United States Copyright Act without the permission
of the copyright owner is unlawful. Requests for
permission or further information should be addressed to
the Permissions Department, John Wiley & Sons, Inc.

This publication is designed to provide accurate and
authoritative information in regard to the subject
matter covered. It is sold with the understanding that
the publisher is not engaged in rendering legal, accounting,
or other professional services. If legal advice or other
expert assistance is required, the services of a competent
professional person should be sought. *From a Declaration
of Principles jointly adopted by a Committee of the
American Bar Association and a Committee of Publishers.*

Library of Congress Cataloging-in-Publication Data

Messersmith, Ann M.
  Forecasting in foodservice / Ann M. Messersmith, Judy L. Miller.
    p.   cm.
  Includes bibliographical references and index.
  ISBN 0-471-52916-8
    1. Food service—Planning.   2. Food service—Forecasting.
  I. Miller, Judy L.   II. Title.
  TX911.3.P46M47   1991
  647.95'0112—dc20   91-3729

Printed in the United States of America

10 9 8 7 6 5 4 3 2 1

ACKNOWLEDGMENTS

S incere appreciation is expressed to Agnes Ferngren, secretary in the Nutrition and Food Management Department at Oregon State University, for the many hours spent in the production of this book. An abundant amount of time was spent "after hours" to help with the preparation of the text, tables, and illustration coordination. Melvin Yost, graphic artist at Oregon State University prepared the figures. The assistance of these two people made the book possible.

Ongoing mentoring and technical writing techniques by Marian Spears, Ph.D., R.D., textbook author and Professor Emeritus, Kansas State University, is greatly appreciated. We wish to acknowledge and thank Oregon State University and Kansas State University for supporting the book. Many thanks to faculty and staff who encouraged and supported the development of the text.

PREFACE

Forecasting in Foodservice was written to assist all foodservice operations to strengthen customer satisfaction and to enhance "bottom line" results. Service is a focus in the foodservice industry, and forecasting menu items is one method of satisfying customers by meeting quantity and quality demand. Under- or over-production can be controlled through forecasting methods; this translates directly to cost control, something of prime importance to the foodservice industry in all economic climates.

The dynamic foodservice industry in commercial and non-commercial arenas includes such varied operations as double drive-through and destination restaurants, school foodservice, in-store feeding, and foodservice for the transportation and health care industries. Each can use forecasting methods to plan production of their menu mix. The reduced cost resulting from accurate forecasting methods has been documented by research. Forecasting is a technique that can assist food managers in running an organization that is accountable, profitable, and provides continuous quantity and quality improvement. Food managers surveyed in studies have indicated the need for improvement and additional training in the area of forecasting.

The forecasting methods developed in this book can be used with manual or computer techniques. The entire application of a forecasting method is presented for manual implementation. In the last chapter, the use of a computer in forecasting is discussed. Recipe adjustment methods are presented in Appendix A. Mini case studies, providing additional forecasting exercises for students and practitioners, are included in Appendix B.

Although all foodservice operations function with some type of forecasting, the theory persists that a formal method can enhance the forecasts. Through better forecasts, both food and service can be improved. Food managers can assess and improve the existing forecasting method in their operations by using the guidelines identified in this book.

ANN M. MESSERSMITH, PhD, RD

JUDY L. MILLER, PhD, RD

August 1991

CONTENTS

Forecasting in Foodservice

1

FORECASTING: IMPACT ON FOOD PRODUCTION MANAGEMENT

orecasting is a very important ongoing function in food management. It is possibly the most valuable function following the menu, which is the *key* to the food production operation. The results of forecasting may actually assist the menu development as an in-depth review of actual menu item choices made by customers at each meal. Forecasting is the technique and skill of identifying the amount of food to be prepared for the customer. The accuracy with which the forecast is made has a direct impact on the food quantity and costs. Therefore, it affects the financial bottom line or well-being of the organization.

The impact of forecasting on food production management can be great. The forecasting function has an effect on many components contributing to the overall success of the foodservice. Some of the components to be managed are:

1. Production volume
2. Costs of under- and over-forecasts
3. Personnel pride
4. Managers' confidence
5. Customer satisfaction.

Therefore, the organization of the forecast information in this book is directed to consider these components.

FORECASTING DEFINED

Over the years, food production operations have always used some type of forecasting. In some operations, it is called *ordering* in which a skilled foodservice person determines how much of each menu item is needed for customer meals. Ordering may be referred to as prediction or forecast. A *prediction* is an estimated quantity of food using subjective information often from the memory of an experienced foodservice person.

Forecasting is defined as a technique for utilizing past information in a systematic way to estimate future needs. It is a planning function or tool for production that can be used by the manager in estimating the amount of food to prepare, scheduling equipment, and planning labor for the preparation and service of food for the customer.

Forecasts for menu item production are the result of an estimate for the future based on past data, actual service quantities, or sales results. Forecasts directly affect functions other than production such as purchasing, equipment use, personnel scheduling, and expected sales. The food production unit has a mixture of complex food production techniques. Some of the menu items such as cakes, frozen entrees, and proportioned beverages are purchased fully prepared; others require complicated prepreparation as well as preparation with sophisticated equipment and highly skilled personnel. A quantitative forecasting method permits time and other resources to be more efficiently used in the actual production unit. Accurate information generated with a forecast helps to control the quantity, quality, and cost of the menu items.

This book serves as a guide for the food manager in developing a forecasting method that will be a result of an operation procedure rather than being dependent on a skilled person to accomplish the task. The forecasting methods that will be discussed can be used with or without the aid of a *computer*.

FORECASTER'S RESPONSIBILITY

In the past, the good forecaster was a person who could be the most accurate in determining customer menu item selections. This individual bore the responsibility for forecasting amounts of menu items that allowed cooks to feel secure in preparing these amounts. Some forecasters felt the pressure of "not running out" so strongly that they over-forecast. Over-forecasting led to leftover or wasted food and under-forecasting led to food that ran out before customer demand was satisfied.

Over-forecasting leading to over-production does not cause personnel stress at the service time because cooks, service employees, and managers are assured that the customer will receive their menu choices. The problem with over-forecasting, thus over-production, is the cost of unused prepared food. Some of the food can be planned into another day's menu. Many menu items, however, have to be discarded if not used, such as fresh vegetable salads, grilled sandwiches, casserole entrees, breads, and some desserts. A second cost is the labor associated with handling, such as wrapping and storing, recording, replanning; and finally, the quality of leftover food deteriorates rapidly. Costs of rehandling and discarding menu items is high, but is rarely calculated, thus becoming a hidden cost.

Under-forecasting leads to running out of menu items—more immediate concerns—and causes high stress to cooks, service employees, and managers. More important, customers do not receive their menu choices. Assigning a dollar value to under-forecasting is difficult. What is the cost of losing a customer, or of substituting a higher priced menu item? What are personnel costs associated with crises decisions in which production or service strategy should be considered? Generally, cooks, service employees, and managers are all involved in solving the problem of menu item shortage. Because this is extremely stressful, forecasters are likely to make the decision to over-forecast. They believe having too much food is better than running out. This over-forecast can range from a few to as many as 50 percent of the menu items in some operations.

The forecasting methods described in this book include not only the use of professional decisions, but also include a mathematical method to incorporate past customer records into decisions. The forecasting method that is detailed will assist the food management operations team in planning a forecasting procedure that has the capability of reducing over-and under-production, as well as relieving the current forecaster from some of the job stresses.

FORECASTING TEAM

Traditionally, one person has been responsible for forecasting in a food operation. A cook, however, may become involved if the forecast made by the forecaster is believed not to be accurate, resulting in the cook making adjustments. Other times, managers might change a forecast. In each instance, even though the decision to change might have been necessary, the adjusted forecast often is found to be in error and seldom is recorded. As a result, forecasting records may not be accurate, giving poor data from which to base future forecasts for planning food production.

Four foodservice operations persons have responsibility for forecasting. For the purpose of this book, they are titled: food manager, head cook, data recorder, and forecaster (see Figure 1.1).

Foodservice Manager: A person who has responsibility for management of the entire food production.

Head Cook: A technically skilled person responsible for preparing menu items for the customer.

Data Recorder: A person who is responsible for the food production records.

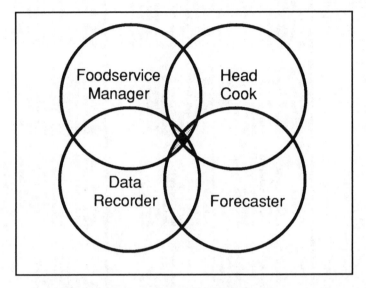

Figure 1.1 Forecasting team.

Forecaster: A person with responsibility to final-
ize the forecasts.

In some foodservice organizations, management,
cooking, recording, and forecasting functions may be the
responsibility of one, two, three, or more people. Responsibilities will vary in title and tasks within organizations or
the development of a forecasting method.

FOOD PRODUCTION UNIT

The food production unit in a foodservice operation is the
area where menu items are prepared for the customer. This
unit or area involves many interrelated functions driven by
menu that are affected by forecasting. The menu controls
all activities in the production unit. Forecasting generates
the estimated quantities of menu items needed to meet

Menu

September 16-22, 1990

	sunday	monday	tuesday	wednesday	thursday	friday	saturday
breakfast	Orange-68 or Apple-80 Juice / Scrambled Eggs w/Ham-208 / Tater Tots-207 / Fresh Fruit Bowl-75 / French Coffee Cake-295 / Assorted Cold Cereal / Toast, Jelly, Beverage / Donuts-124	Orange-68 or Grapefruit -62 Juice / Malt-O-Meal-67 / Waffles-240 w/Syrup-98 / Bacon-85 / Poached Eggs-82 each / Assorted Cold Cereal / Toast, Jelly, Beverage	Orange Juice-68 or Cranberry Cocktail-98 / Ralston-72 / Fried Eggs-85 each / Sausage Patty-141 / Mixed Fruit Pieces-85 / Blueberry Buckle-301 / Assorted Cold Cereal / Toast, Jelly, Beverage	Orange-68 or Grape-76 Juice / Rice & Raisins-84 / French Toast-216 w/ Syrup-98 / Canadian Bacon-50 / Hard or Soft Cooked Eggs -68 each / Honey Wheat Muffins-312 / Assorted Cold Cereal / Toast, Jelly, Beverage	Orange-68 or Pineapple -95 Juice / Farina-67 / Scrambled Eggs-168 / Bacon-85 / Criss Cut Potatoes-142 / Harvest Sweet Rolls-353 / Assorted Cold Cereal / Toast, Jelly, Beverage	Orange-68 or V-8 -31 Juice / Pettijohns-70 / Chipped Beef Gravy-222 over Corn Bread-195 / Fried Eggs-85 each / Grape Cluster-71 / Corn Bread-195 w/ Honey-61 / Assorted Cold Cereal / Toast, Jelly, Beverage	Orange-68 or Assorted Juices / Eggs Grilled to Order-170 / Ham Slice-47 / Blueberries w/ Cream-77 / Danish Coffee Cake -279 / Assorted Cold Cereal / Toast, Jelly, Beverage
lunch	Roast Turkey Breast-116 / Apple Pancakes-382 w/Syrup-98 & Sausage Links-270 / Parsley Seasoned Potatoes -131 / Seasoned Peas-54 / Calabacita-95 / Golden Prairie Popcorn Rolls-115 / Italian Cream Cake-315 / Ice Cream-133 / Fresh Fruit-80	Beef Noodle Casserole-387 / Oriental Luncheon Plate -475 / Cream of Vegetable Soup -89 / German Carrots-51 / Vanilla Pudding-175 / Popsicle-95 / Fresh Fruit-80	Ham & Cheese Hoagie-360 w/Chips-78 / California Casserole-254 / Country Turkey Soup-47 / Fordhook Lima Beans-73 / Whole Wheat Sugar Cookies-257 / Ice Milk Bar-144 / Fresh Fruit-80	Beef French Dip Sandwich -394 / Ginger Fruit Freeze Salad Plate-435 / Cream of Potato Soup-152 / Fruit Punch-82 / Gingersnaps-286 / Raspberry Sherbet-118 / Fresh Fruit-80	Cavatini-228 / Brighten a Bluebery Day Salad Plate-618 / Beef Noodle Soup-122 / Banana Scallops-126 / Chocolate Chip Cookies -394 / Fudgesicle-91 / Fresh Fruit-80	Corn Dogs-319 each w/Chips-78 / Tuna Noodle Casserole -259 / Plaza III Soup-122 / Chilled Apple Juice-90 / Tua Tua Cookies-286 / Ice Cream Sandwich-167 / Fresh Fruit-80	Turkey & Dumplings-334 / Chef's Salad Plate-295 / Italian Sausage Soup -77 / Seasoned Cauliflower -17 / Golden Oatmeal Cookies-318 / Creamsicle-103 / Fresh Fruit-80
dinner	Chicken Fillet on Bun w/ Lettuce & Tomato-310 / Salisbury Steak-276 w/Mushroom Gravy-51 / Southern Style Hash Browns-164 / Broccoli Spears-24 / Wax Beans-23 / Hot Rolls-114 / Devil's Food Cake-275 w/ Mocha Fudge Frosting-92 / Chilled Pineapple-77	Chicken Fried Steak-330 / Grilled Bratwurst on Bun -558 w/Bavarian Sauerkraut-25 / Whipped Potatoes-113 w/ Cream Gravy-75 / Corn on the Cob-90 / Tomatoes w/Croutons-127 / Rye Rolls-107 / Pumpkin Pie-274 / Chilled Boysenberries-36		BBQ Ribs-126 / Breaded Shrimp-331 / Riel Biel-100 / Cut Green Beans-23 / Stir Fried Vegetables-62 / Egg Dinner Rolls-125 / Peach Cobbler-217 / Chilled Cherries-51	COWBOY CLASSICS DINNER / "Rawhide" Beef Steak-365 / "Boot Hill" Baked Potato -287 / "Bonanza" Baked Beans-60 / Ben Cartright Corn-61 / Butch Cassidy Biscuits -254 w/Honey Butter-99 & Honey-61 / Sundance Kid Shortcake -408 / "Big Valley" Berry Bowl-40	SUB "N" SUNDAE / Roast Pork Loin-216 / Chicken Fajita-345 / Potatoes Romanoff-341 / Mixed Vegetables-41 / Curried Pear Halves-47 / Hot Rolls-114 / Ice Cream Cones / Assorted Chilled Fruit -65	AWAY FOOTBALL GAME: / NORTHERN ILLINOIS - 6:35 P.M. / Cheese Manicotti w/ Meat Sauce-412 / Celery Almondine-47 / Seasoned Peas-54 / French Bread-88 / Lemon Supreme Dessert-352 / Chilled Mixed Fruit -111

Salad bar served daily at lunch and dinner.
Unforeseeable circumstances may cause menu items to change.

Figure 1.2 Menu exhibit. Numbers following the menu item indicate file code. (Used by permission of Kansas State University Residence Hall Foodservice, Manhattan, Kansas.)

the customer selections. Four components are directly affected by the forecast: (1) menu, (2) recipes, (3) production worksheet/schedule, and (4) forecast. A description of each follows:

Menu: A planned list of menu items from which the customer may select a meal. *The menu item selection quantities are used as information for generating future forecasts.* (See Figure l.2.)

Recipe: Document that identifies the menu item name, volume, preparation time, as well as the list and amount of ingredients and methods of preparation. *Forecasts indicate how many servings of the menu items are needed.* (see Figure l.3.)

Production Worksheet Schedule: Person, quantity, yield, directions, and time required for preparing menu items. *Forecast indicates number of servings* for each menu item, thus providing basic information for production scheduling. (See Figure 1.4.)

Forecast: Number of customers selecting the menu items prepared in the production unit. *Forecast provides an estimate of the number of customers expected to select each menu item.* (See Tables 1.1 and 1.2.)

FORECASTING RESULTS

The emphasis on forecasting in a foodservice organization depends upon the philosophy of the management. The most rewarding results of an accurate forecast are customer satisfaction, personnel pride and job satisfaction, manager

```
LEMON CHICKEN                    RECIPE CODE - 16-25-1-085-3        STATUS - DEVELOPMENTAL    2

  / /    -******-       ****************************************
                                 ***NUMBER OF PORTIONS              50
EQUIPMENT-STEAM JACKETED KETTLE     PORTION SIZE/COST               181 LBS.          /    $0.4386
         FRENCH WHIP                MEAL PATTERN ALLOWANCE          ONE PORTION
         DEEP FAT FRYER             SUGGESTED SERVING UTENSIL       SPOON
                                    PAN SIZE                        12x20x2
                                    NUMBER OF PANS                     1
                                    WEIGHT PER PAN                   8.50 LBS.
                                    HANDLING LOSS                   15.00 PERCENT
                                    MINIMUM BATCH
RECIPE SOURCE-KSU 4/88              MAXIMUM BATCH
                                    FORECAST UNIT
03/05/90  4.13 PM     900305        TOTAL RECIPE WEIGHT/COST        10.6 LBS.         /    $21.9300
                                    TOTAL RECIPE VOLUME
```

CODE	PERCENT	INGREDIENT	WEIGHTS AND MEASURES	AP/EP	STEP	PROCEDURE
0082021058	4.58	CORNSTARCH 100 LBS	0.49 LBS		A	1. COMBINE IN STEAM JACKETED KETTLE.
0082093008	12.73	SUGAR GRANULATED	1.4 LBS			BLEND WITH FRENCH WHIP.
0082033005	9.43	VINEGAR CIDER	1.0 LBS		B	2. ADD. STIR UNTIL SMOOTH WITH FRENCH WHIP.
0000000001	31.59	WATER	3.4 LBS			
0063010461	11.32	FZN LEMON JUICE RECONSTITUTED	1.2 LBS			
0082061505	0.05	GINGER GROUND	1.0 TSP		C	3. ADD. BLEND IN. COOK AND STIR UNTIL MIXTURE IS TRANSLUCENT.
0082052506	0.09	LEMON PEEL	2.9 TSP			
0082080208	0.85	SOUP BASE CHICKEN	0.09 LBS			
0082061408	0.19	GARLIC POWDER	0.02 LBS			
0082063401	0.05	PEPPER WHITE GROUND	1.0 TSP			
0082030057	5.66	CATSUP CND	0.60 LBS			
0041002105	4.72	OIL SALAD 5 GAL	0.50 LBS			
0082093504	14.15	SYRUP WHITE	1.5 LBS			
0082032009	4.58	SOY SAUCE	0.49 LBS			
0013167707	117.39	CHICKEN NIBBLETS	12.5 LBS	X	D	4. DEEP FAT FRY AT 350 DEG.F. FOR 3-4 MINUTES OR UNTIL DONE.
						5. PLACE 5.0 LBS IN 12x20x2 INCH PAN.
						6. POUR 3.5 LBS OF SAUCE OVER CHICKEN. STIR GENTLY TO COAT.
						7. ONE PORTION IS 0.25 LBS OF CHICKEN PLUS 0.181 LBS OF SAUCE (0.431 LBS TOTAL).

Figure 1.3 Recipe sample: Computer-generated recipe. (Used by permission of Kansas State University Residence Hall Foodservice, Manhattan, Kansas.)

Residence Hall Foodservice
PRODUCTION SCHEDULE

Unit ___ Main Production

Date ___ 1/24/90

Meal: Bkf. ___ Lunch _X_ Dinner ___

Meal Count 2153 Weather Fair Comments Basketball Game

EMPLOYEE	MENU ITEM	QUANTITY TO PREPARE	ACTUAL YIELD	INSTRUCTIONS	TIME SCHEDULE	LEFT OVER AMOUNT	RUN OUT TIME	SUBSTITUTION	CLEANING ASSIGNMENT
Vege	Country Fried Steak	1200	1220	Use 2 Tilting Fry Pans and	Begin frying 2:15 See Frying Time schedule	35 servings	--	--	Whatley-- Tilting fry pans
Whatley				oven number 3					
Lundin	Giant Rolled Tostados	1000	1020	Serve open face on cafeteria line and clientele will roll their own.		50 tortillas 10 lbs meat mixture 1 gal cheese sce.	--	--	Lundin-- slicer and attachments
McCurdy	Whipped Potatoes	1200	1150	If necessary use instant as a back up	Begin steaming potatoes at 3:00	12 lbs	--	--	
McCurdy	Cream Gravy	2000	1600	Make 4 batches 600--600--400--400 (if needed) Serve over both steak and potatoes		2 gal	--	--	
Vege	Mexican Rice	900	900	Use 12 x 10 x 4 pans	See Baking Time schedule	18 lbs	--	--	
Mockery	Refried Beans	850	850	Add bean liquid as needed to maintain a moist product		12 lbs	--	--	Mockery-- Oven number 1, shelves and doors
Mockery	Broccoli Spears	1000	850	Season with melted margarine	Begin 4:00 Prepare based on demand	0	6:00	2½ lbs Asparagus Spears	
Mockery	Yogurt Cup	20	20	Serve whole container--blueberry, cherry, rum raisin, plain		8	--	--	

PRE PREPARATION:

EMPLOYEE	MENU ITEM	QUANTITY	INSTRUCTIONS
McCurdy	Roast Beef	600 lbs	Pan beef in baking pans, cover and refrigerate
Mockery	Hard Cooked Eggs	5 doz.	For garnish on spinach

EMPLOYEE	MENU ITEM	QUANTITY	INSTRUCTIONS
Lundin	(Omelet) fresh eggs	1 case	Break into 60 qt mixer bowl
Vege	Ham	10 lbs	Dice for omelets

Figure 1.4 Production schedule. (Used by permission of Kansas State University Residence Hall Foodservice, Manhattan, Kansas, and Spears, M. C.: *Foodservice Organizations: A Managerial and Systems Approach*, (New York: Macmillan, 1991).

Table 1.1   Menu Cycle Forecast Record (Excerpt)

Menu Cycle: Winter			Menu Item Cycle Data Record			
Date	Day	Menu	Forecast	Actual Demand	Forecast Error	Length of Time if Product Outage (Minutes)
02/04/91	Mon	Lasagna	462	430	32	
02/11/91	Mon	Lasagna	445	440	5	
02/18/91	Mon	Lasagna	443	439	4	
02/25/91	Mon	Lasagna	442	442	0	5 minutes

Table 1.2   Daily Forecast Record (Excerpt)

			Menu Item per Meal			
Date	Day	Menu	Forecast	Actual Demand	Forecast Error	Length of Time if Product Outage (Minutes)
02/04/91	Mon	Lasagna	462	430	32	
02/04/91	Mon	Pork chop	162	143	19	
02/04/91	Mon	White fish fillet	245	230	15	
02/04/91	Mon	Chef salad	85	80	5	
02/04/91	Mon	Green beans	290	290	0	20 minutes
02/04/91	Mon	Stir fry vegetables	580	549	31	
02/04/91	Mon	Harvard beets	80	80	0	5 minutes

confidence, operational controls, and profit or breakeven financial status.

Customer satisfaction is one of the most important results of an accurate forecast method and a well-managed production operation. The consistent benefit of not running out of food items is a confidence builder for the personnel of the production unit. Also, this confidence can be reflected in positive marketing and overall image of the foodservice establishment to the customer. Customers can be members of the general public in a restaurant or members of special catered parties; students in a university; patients in a hospital; visitors to a resort or club; travelers on an airline, train, or bus; long-term inmates in a prison; residents in health care facilities; children and adults in day care centers; workers in business and industry; and family members eating meals away from home.

Personnel pride and job satisfaction occur in the food production area if menu items meet quality standards and are available when the customer wants to eat a meal. The personnel tension or stress within the work areas is likely to be reduced when the quantities of food items to produce are at an accuracy level that results in opportunities to have a well-run production area. Satisfied personnel also serve as an indirect marketing agent and continue to share their work satisfaction with family and friends. A forecasting method that is accurate will contribute to personnel pride and job satisfaction.

Manager confidence is attained when the manager, as a member of the food production team, has a unique position in the foodservice organization of—he or she is in charge, having the overall responsibility for production. An accurate forecasting method will provide information for managing scarce resources, thus improving the bottom line and accountability.

Operational accuracy is attained when forecast records are used as an operational tool in a well-structured production unit. As earlier stated, the menu is the first and most important record in the foodservice operation; the next most important records are forecast records and recipes. The forecast estimating the amount of food to order, prepare, and serve directly affects recipe quantities and general production loads. Other important records are production work sheets and cost documents, each influenced by forecast quantities.

Profitable financial status is enhanced or improved with forecasting control. With control, over- and under-production costs are minimized with reduced chances of preparing too much or too little of the menu items. One food production operation calculated costs of over-and under-production to be an average of $1,215 in a seven-day period in 1973.* When the forecasts are in control, food production personnel can take advantage of the time required for solving over-and under-production problems, thus reducing labor costs. Other costs of over-production also can be controlled, such as food waste, inventory record keeping for over-produced food, and supplies for packaging the food for storage. Under-production causes customer dissatisfaction and loss, higher food cost of substituted items, and personnel labor cost and stress.

PLAN FOR FORECASTING SUCCESS

The mission of the production area is to provide the customer with an excellent menu item at the least cost. The forecasting method can help the forecaster to achieve this mission through customers, personnel satisfaction, manager confidence, operation controls, and profit.

* Messersmith, A. M., Moore, A. N., and Hoover, L. W., "A Multi-Echelon Menu Item Forecasting System for Hospitals," *Journal of the American Dietetic Association* 72:509, May, 1978.

Planning for a forecasting method takes time and management team work. The team generally includes the forecaster, manager, head cook, and data recorder. The organizational philosophy of the food management team must include developing and implementing a forecast method, as well as maintaining an active role in better management methods, menus, and recipes.

Operational activities in the foodservice management organization need to be reviewed. Records, which include recipes, production sheets, and cost data, are key documents that are involved in forecasting. The sequence or flow of information should be in a logical, workable order. In some food operations, these records need updating, revising, or resequencing not only to enable forecasting but also to make available to personnel the most current, efficient, and accurate records. In a new food production facility, these records can be created at the same time that the forecasting method is being developed.

Success of the food production operation will be due partly to the accurate and current record documentation of the operation functions. Personnel knowledge and support, as well as efficient facility design and purchasing techniques also enhance the possibility of success. Forecasting impacts much of the success of the other foodservice production functions. The data collection, organization, and evaluation is helpful in managing the food production operation. The preparation process for forecasting alone leads to better management.

Allocating resources is a task for which the manager of the foodservice operation is responsible. The manager needs to review resources in an existing facility to determine how procedures might be changed or personnel can be retrained to plan and implement an updated forecasting method. The management team that is involved in forecasting should be able to rearrange labor time for forecasting implementation. The foodservice manager should plan the overall method and evaluate the operation for any new techniques needed. If production operation records are not available or need extensive revision, perhaps an additional person could be budgeted for the planning and implementation phases. However, the forecasting method, once implemented, should fit into the operation without additional resources. In most cases, the person doing the current forecasting—the forecaster—should work with the new method in conjunction with the foodservice manager, head cook, and data recorder.

WRAP UP

An accurate forecast leads to reduced costs in the production unit of a foodservice operation. The planning, implementation, and use of forecasting can be viewed as a positive effort toward efficient management. Outcomes or results are reflected in many ways, such as less expensive food and labor costs, satisfied customers and employees, and improved overall management. Although additional resources are not required for the development and use of a forecasting system, reallocation of existing resources, however, will be needed. Record keeping may have to be modified to make forecast data more available.

ACTION

Actions needed by the foodservice manager to forecast menu items are summarized below:

1. Select a forecasting team consisting of a foodservice manager, forecaster, head cook, and data recorder and identify a team leader.

2. Discuss the concept of updating the forecasting method and review anticipated results.

3. Review the current forecasting method and evaluate the data accuracy.

4. Study and revise, if necessary, the menu, recipes, production scheduling, and customer choices of menu items. Each of the documents must be current and contain accurate information including dates, days of week, menu item forecast, and the amount actually sold or customer demand.

5. Revise food production documents, if needed, or establish some draft documents, such as menu, recipes, production schedules, and customer choices or sales information to enhance the forecasting method.

REFERENCES

Messersmith, A. M., Moore, A. N., and Hoover, L. W., "A Multi-Echelon Menu Item Forecasting System for Hospitals," *Journal of the American Dietetic Association 72*:509, May, 1978.

Spears, M. C., *Foodservice Organizations,* 2d ed. (New York: Macmillan, 1991).

West, B., West, L., Harger, V. F., Shugart, G. S., and Payne-Palacio, J., *Foodservice in Institutions,* 6th ed. (New York: Macmillan, 1988).

2

FORECASTING: DATA REVIEW

T he forecaster of menu items needs accurate and clearly recorded production information from the foodservice production unit. During the time a forecasting method is being developed in the foodservice, a review of production records and possible update of operations can be made. Operational records to review include menus, production worksheets/ schedules, and recipes. In addition, the methods of forecasting currently being used should be re-evaluated for inclusion in the revised method. Personnel are also a major resource to the foodservice and forecasting function. Reorganization or retraining of personnel may be required to establish and implement a forecasting method; an increase of personnel is generally not anticipated.

Prepare to develop a forecasting method by reviewing current foodservice records. Also, data, or the factual information in records, must be reviewed for accuracy. Data are the basis of the forecasting method, providing important information for management decision making.

FOODSERVICE RECORDS REVIEW

Because forecasting uses past information in a systemized way to estimate future needs, it is a *planning function* that is based on production records of the foodservice. The accuracy of the forecast depends upon the availability and validity of the records.

Few managers have had time to oversee the analysis and use of past data; therefore, the foodservice lacks a systemized forecasting method. As a result, only the most recent records and knowledge of the forecaster get used to generate a menu item forecast for the next food order or production worksheet/schedule. Often, recent records will reflect an unusual event that will not occur again, thus giving an inaccurate forecast. A much more accurate forecast can be made by using all past data (including recent data) to establish a pattern that has developed over time. By using a forecasting method that requires these data, forecasts with a minimum number of errors can be computed.

The forecasting method detailed in this book is a systematic method in which useful data are taken from operational records and sorted according to same menu item, day of the week, and/or meal. These data provide the forecaster with information to make operational and service decisions regarding amounts of menu items needed in the future. The forecaster does not have to be a statistician or a computer programmer to use this method effectively. This forecasting method, as with any new or modified major function, will require some change in the foodservice operation and personnel training. Operational data to be used by the forecaster is described next.

Menu

The menu is an operational tool that influences purchasing, production, and service functions. One key control is to have menus that are as standard as possible, although variations can be accommodated. The *menu* is a collection of food items from which customers select their meal. The popularity of each menu item influences the forecast and, therefore, production. For example, chicken may be more popular than a casserole and will therefore be selected more often. However, a steak sandwich in combination with chicken, may be as popular as the chicken by itself. Whatever the case, a menu that is satisfactory and doesn't change too often provides a basis for a more accurate forecast. Demand data are the number of menu item servings or portions that were actually selected and purchased by the customer.

The forecasting method for food production assumes that the same days of the week generally have the same number of customers, which is identified as customer demand. Likewise, menu item choices by customers for the same days, defined as menu item demand, will be similar.

The same menus, over a long period of time, become boring to customers; therefore, foodservice personnel and astute managers often make changes. Each time menu items are changed, however, past demand data lose accuracy. When changes occur, some adjustment of the forecast method may be needed to restore the same level of accuracy. A *cycle menu* is a series of menus offering different items daily on a weekly, biweekly, or some other basis, after which the cycle is repeated. A one-day static menu, often referred to as a *restaurant menu,* is repeated daily. A two-week cycle consists of two weeks of menus that repeats.

As stated earlier, the menu is the key record from which all other foodservice activities are developed. Two types of menus are single and multiple choices. The *single choice,* or no choice, provides the customer with no choice in menu items. In this type of menu, all customers receive the same menu item. The customer's only choice is whether or not to eat the menu items; therefore, only customer demand would need to be forecast. A single choice menu would be typical at some camps, catered banquets, prisons, or health care foodservices. Customer count data can be collected from enrollment, pre-sold meal tickets, point of sale, or census data. These records, including date, day of week, and meal (breakfast, lunch, or dinner), need to be *saved.* An example of a single-choice menu is illustrated in Figure 2.1.

A selective or *multiple choice* menu has more than one menu item in each category from which the customer can choose. Menus generally have six categories: (1) appetizer, (2) entree, (3) potato or substitute, (4) vegetables, (5) salads, and (6) dessert, as shown in Figure 2.2. In foodservice operations with selective menus, two forecasts would be required: customer demand and menu item demand.

Sandwich Buffet

Roast Beef and Cheese Sandwich

Spinach Salad with
    Hot Bacon Dressing

Melon Cup

Coffee, Tea, Milk

Figure 2.1 Single choice menu for a catered luncheon.

```
Cream of Broccoli Cheese Soup
Tomato Juice


Baked Chicken Breast with Orange Sauce
Shrimp and Scallop Stir-fry with Vegetables


Steamed Rice
Pan Roasted Potatoes


Peas Almandine
Sauteed Mushrooms


Fresh Green Salad or
Sliced Tomato Salad
        Blue Cheese Dressing
        French Dressing
        Oil and Vinegar Low Calorie Dressing
        Russian Low Calorie Dressing


Pound Cake with Raspberries
Pineapple Sherbet
```

Figure 2.2   Selective or multiple choice menu for a dinner meal.

The manager needs to know the projected number of customers and the percentage choosing each menu item within a category.

If the organization has more than one menu cycle for each day, forecasts should be done for each cycle. For example, a hospital foodservice with a *one-day* restaurant-type menu for patient meal service, a *two-week cycle* for the cafeteria, and a *special events menu* would need three forecasts daily. If the same menu item is on each of the three menus, then the three forecasts can be combined. Menu development is a function that demands professional expertise and care. Much time is required to produce menus that meet customers' needs and that are cost-effective. Often forecast data such as menu item demand reflect poor menu planning. Having one very unpopular menu item really is not offering a choice to the majority of the customers.

Prior to generating a forecast, several like days of menu item totals should be collected. A sample record of a two-week menu cycle entree item, chicken and club sandwich, is shown in Table 2.1. This record contains the day, date, menu item, and menu item demand for the entrees, as well as the total number of customers for the observed meal. A

Table 2.1 Two-Week Menu Cycle
Record for Tuesday Entree and Menu Item Demand

Day	Date	Menu Item	Menu Item Demand	Total Customers for the Meal
Tue	06/05/90	Chicken	120	275
Tue	06/19/90	Chicken	140	250
Tue	07/03/90	Chicken	135	263
Tue	06/05/90	Club Sandwich	80	275
Tue	06/19/90	Club Sandwich	100	250
Tue	07/03/90	Club Sandwich	93	263

column for the forecast menu item amount can also be added if these data are available.

Production Worksheets

The production worksheet, often referred to as a *production schedule,* is the document that translates menu items into a production plan. The production worksheet contains guidelines and plans for the cooks to use in preparing meals. A worksheet should be prepared for each day's menu items and should include the following information:

- Menu item name
- Employee name
- Quantity to prepare
- Preparation instructions
- Preparation time schedule
- Special instructions
- Actual yield
- Over- and under-production data
- Substitutions for under-production.

In this list of information categories, the *quantity to prepare* is the *forecast* for each menu item. The food production unit may have one, two, or more worksheets. Most operations have a Cold Food Production Worksheet that includes salads, sandwiches, and pre-preparation food items such as onions, celery, or other cold foods and one for Hot Food Production that includes soup, vegetables, and entrees. In some operations, a worksheet for desserts as well as beverages is used. See Table 2.2 for an excerpt of a production worksheet. Even though broiled salmon is the only illustration, each menu item should be included in the daily production worksheet.

Table 2.2 Production Worksheet Excerpt

Date: June

Day: Tuesday

Menu Cycle: Summer

Expected Number of Customers:[a] 400

Employee	Menu Item	Time Needed	Amount to Prepare[b]	Actual Yield	Leftover	Amount Used[c]	Time and Special Directions	Under-Production Substitution
Cook I	Broiled salmon	11:30 A.M.	200 serv.	185	15	170	Begin cooking at 11:15 A.M.	—

[a] Expected number of customers = forecast of customer demand
[b] Amount to prepare = forecast of menu item demand
[c] Amount used = menu item demand

The production worksheet (see Table 2.2) is one of the data sources for forecasting. Note that an expected *number of customers* for the entire meal, or the *forecast* is recorded at the top of the Worksheet of Customer Demand. In addition, a menu item demand forecast—amount to prepare—for each item as well as the amount used will be needed as forecast data the next time the menu appears. The production worksheet also serves as a record for identifying the substituted menu items that are added in the case of underproduction of the menu item. Forecasting data recorded on the production worksheet—amount to prepare/forecast and the amount used/customer demand—are needed to calculate the difference in these amounts. The calculated difference is the *forecast error,* which is a value that can be quickly referred to by the forecaster to determine the accuracy of the forecast. To calculate the forecast error the following calculation is made:

Forecast Error = Amount to Prepare – Amount Used
      (forecast menu   (menu item
        item demand)   demand)

The forecast minus the actual menu item demand is the forecast error. The forecast or amount to prepare is always the first known value in planning the production. The menu item demand or amount used is the last value learned; that is, it is determined after the meal service. The forecast data are listed first, the menu item demand is second or Forecast Error (FE) is equal to Forecast (F) minus Demand (D); therefore,

$$FE = F - D.$$

At the end of a meal or production period, the person responsible calculates the error or the difference. In the case of customers wanting more than the amount prepared (running out of food item), a negative forecast error would result. A substituted menu item and the time of day the food item ran out should be recorded to indicate the estimated number of servings that were short. As an example, if 225 servings were forecast and they were sold out and 15 servings of a substituted menu item were sold, then the forecast error would reflect an under-forecast.

In the case of hospital foodservice where customers (patients) select the menu item prior to the meal service, there can be more orders (demand) than forecasted. There is therefore an under-production and an under-forecast recorded. This example represents a short period of time when the order is placed and the menu item is served. There is not enough time to produce additional servings of the menu item, thus a substitute is made.

The production worksheet is a very important record, as the planning and production information must be accurate. The responsibility to keep accurate data should be that of the head cook or person responsible for main production.

Recipes

Menu items are produced with the aid of recipes. The recipe should be well-documented to serve as a forecast and production guide. Each recipe should contain three sections of information:

1. Recipe name, portion size, cooking temperature, and time, as well as other information to assist in the product control

2. Ingredient name and amount

3. Procedures for the assembly of the recipe to produce the menu item in the correct amount.

Recipe accuracy is very important to provide the expected number and size of portions. A consistent dependent recipe yield for menu items provides more accurate estimated data for forecasting. Therefore, this section includes format and adjusting methods for recipes. This reference is included to serve as a resource or reminder to the head cook.

An excerpt of a recipe format is shown in Table 2.3. The use of an accurate recipe in which the yield or volume is standardized allows the head cook to *adjust* the volume of the recipe to produce the forecast amount. Adjusting the recipe is a process of increasing or decreasing ingredient amounts to produce the needed volume. Adjusting the recipe can be accomplished by a couple of methods. One method is the *factor method* that was presented by Shugart

Table 2.3   Recipe Form for Quantity Food Production

Product Name: Lemon Sauce
Equipment: Steam Kettle   Yield: 6 quarts
Cooking Time: 20 minutes   Serving information: Serve hot
Pre-Preparation: None   Portion Size: 2 oz
Information: Serve over puddings

Ingredient Code	Ingredient Name	Amount	Procedure
XXXX	Sugar, granulated	4 lb	Mix dry ingredients in cool steam kettle.
XXXX	Salt	1 tsp	
XXXX	Cornstarch	6 oz	
XXXX	Water, hot	8 lb	Add hot water, bring mixture to a boil, and cook slowly until clear (about 20 minutes).
XXXX	Lemon juice	1/2 lb	Add lemon juice and margarine to cooked mixture.
XXXX	Margarine	1/8 lb	

and Molt* (see Appendix A, page 121, for details). This method is based on the volume by weight of the ingredients multiplied by a conversion factor. The conversion factor is obtained by dividing the desired yield by the yield of the original recipe. If 170 servings are forecast, divide 170 by 75, the yield of the original recipe:

$$170 \div 75 = 2.26$$

The 2.26 is the conversion factor. Now, multiply each ingredient weight in the original recipe by 2.26 to obtain the ingredient weight for the new forecast yield. This method allows the recipe to be adjusted, increased, or reduced.

A second method, as documented by Shugart and Molt,[†] for adjusting a recipe is the *percentage method*. In this method, recipe ingredients are also reported in weights. The total weight of ingredients is recorded on the recipe. Each ingredient weight is divided by the total recipe weight giving the *percentage of each ingredient.* Determine the total weight needed by multiplying the portion weight (decimals of a pound) by the number of servings to be prepared. Multiply the total weight by each percentage number to give the exact amount of each ingredient needed. See Appendix A for detailed procedures.

A system to maintain accurate recipes should be routine in all production units. *Standardizing* a recipe is a process that enables the final product to be consistent in quality and permits portion cost control. Standardizing is a major ongoing operational task. Adjusting a recipe with computer-assisted techniques can make this task less burdensome.

---

* Shugart, G., and Molt, N.: *Food for Fifty* 8th ed. (New York: Macmillan, 1989) pp. 53–54.
† *Ibid.,* pp. 54–56.

Standardized recipes are required for accurate forecasting. For example:

> A recipe is adjusted to yield 80 servings, the menu item demand forecast; however, after production, the yield is only 65 servings. In this case, the 80 servings were not produced and a shortage of the menu item occurred. This is not a forecast error, but a recipe or production error. The reason for this shortage may have been ingredient weight miscalculation, larger portion size than planned, possible substituted ingredient, pilferage, or procedure error in producing the menu item. Whatever the problem, it needs to be corrected; the head cook's responsibility is to oversee and monitor production.

Portion size of the menu item must be specified on the recipe, and employees should be trained to use the exact amount of ingredients, follow instructions, and portion the finished product correctly. Dipper and ladle charts, as shown in Tables 2.4 and 2.5, could be used in a training program.

Based on these charts, the portioning or serving utensils should be identified on each recipe. Employees need to understand that cost control depends upon portion control. With the current emphasis on good nutrition, portion control is even more important.

FORECASTING PERSONNEL

Forecasting in a foodservice is maintained by management personnel, a valuable resource. Well trained personnel in every foodservice function is critical for an efficient

Table 2.4   Dipper Equivalents

Dipper* Number	Approximate Measure	Approximate Weight	Suggested Use
6	10 Tbsp (^{2}/$_3$ cup)	6 oz	Entree salads
8	8 Tbsp (^{1}/$_2$ cup)	4–5 oz	Entrees
10	6 Tbsp (^{3}/$_8$ cup)	3–4 oz	Desserts, meat patties
12	5 Tbsp (^{1}/$_3$ cup)	2^1/$_2$–3 oz	Croquettes, vegetables, muffins, desserts, salads
16	4 Tbsp (^{1}/$_4$ cup)	2–2^1/$_4$ oz	Muffins, desserts, croquettes
20	3^1/$_5$ Tbsp	1^3/$_4$–2 oz	Muffins, cupcakes, sauces, sandwich fillings
24	2^2/$_3$ Tbsp	1^1/$_2$–1^3/$_4$ oz	Cream puffs
30	2^1/$_5$ Tbsp	1–1^1/$_2$ oz	Large drop cookies
40	1^1/$_2$ Tbsp	^{3}/$_4$ oz	Drop cookies
60	1 Tbsp	^{1}/$_2$ oz	Small drop cookies, garnishes
100	Scant 2 tsp		Tea cookies

* Portions per quart.

Note: These measurements are based on level dippers. If a rounded dipper is used, the measure and weight are closer to those of the next larger dipper.

Source: Shugart, G., and Molt, M., *Food for Fifty* 8th ed. (New York: Macmillan, 1989).

Table 2.5 Ladle Equivalents

Approximate Measure	Approximate Weight	Suggested Use
⅛ cup	1 oz	Sauces, salad dressings
¼ cup	2 oz	Gravies, some sauces
½ cup	4 oz	Stews, creamed dishes
¾ cup	8 oz	Stews, creamed dishes, soup
1 cup	8 oz	Soup

Note: These measures are based on level ladles. If a rounded ladle is used, the measure is closer to that of the next larger ladle.

Source: Shugart, G., and Molt, M., *Food for Fifty* 8th ed. (New York: Macmillan, 1989).

operation. Forecasting is one of the key functions and the forecaster, data recorder, head cook, foodservice manager, and serving personnel must be initially trained in the forecasting methods. Throughout their employment, they all must be updated on forecasting methods.

Forecasting techniques must be explained to the personnel whose role in the process should be identified. Some foodservice managers just "toss a new technique at personnel" without training or identifying requirements of the new method. An updated forecasting method may take several months to implement fully. However, the implementation can go smoothly with the help of all personnel. The updated method may require modified or new job routines and new data records. In some foodservices, an additional person may be needed to plan, train, and implement the method, depending on the organization structure. Initially, however, the forecasting method should be planned with the original number of personnel with possible reassignment of tasks. All personnel and procedure planning depends on the selected forecasting method including data records to ascertain if change is actually needed. The foodservice manager must evaluate personnel skills, as well as operational techniques.

PRODUCTION INFORMATION

Production and forecasting data must be reviewed to determine the customer and menu item demands from meal to meal and day to day. To do this review, the foodservice manager, forecaster, and data recorder should identify the type of menu items, customer count or sales, to be used as the basis for forecasting.

What Information to Forecast

One or more of the following should be selected for forecasting: food or supplies purchasing, menu item production, revenue, or number of customers. Selecting what to forecast will depend on the foodservice operation. Some factors to consider are the cost of the inventory and storage, over- and under-menu item production, and cash flow. These decisions depend upon the size and complexity of the operation. A fast food or quick service restaurant would forecast for purchasing and the number of food items to prepare for specific time periods throughout the day. A university foodservice would forecast the amount of food to purchase and the amount of each menu item to prepare for each meal. The volume of business in a full scale restaurant would have to be forecast before forecasting the amount of food to purchase and produce as well as the number of employees to schedule.

In each operation, records of menu items sold or the amount of food purchased need to be summarized. For example, Wednesday sales of a particular menu item in a fast food or quick service restaurant are shown in Table 2.6. The number of servings of pancakes sold for the recorded

Table 2.6   Pancake Sales for
Wednesday Breakfast

Date, 1990	Servings Sold
June 06	300
June 13	340
June 20	333
June 27	298
July 04	475
July 11	330

six Wednesdays provides the forecasting team with data for calculating a forecast for future Wednesdays. Holiday demand data usually is tabulated separately as shown in Table 2.7 for July 4th. The number of servings of pancakes sold on a holiday may be higher or lower than normal.

Records of menu items sold provide information to the foodservice manager, forecaster, and cooks in determining the number of servings to produce on future Wednesdays or July 4th.

Table 2.7   July 4th Pancake
Sales for Breakfast

July 4, Year	Servings Sold
1983	300
1984	330
1985	350
1986	350
1987	380
1988	475
1989	460
1990	475

Building a Database

A cycle menu whether for one day or one or more weeks provides an excellent database for forecasting because it is repetitive. The person responsible for forecasting can be trained to tabulate the demand for each menu item. Most cycle menus are selective, thus permitting the customer a choice of menu items in each category. For example in Figure 2.3, the customer can choose one kind of juice or fruit from a list of three. In a foodservice operation using a selective menu, demand data for *each* menu item needs to be collected. A minimum of three observations (data) for each menu item should be collected. The recommendation is that the demand data be recorded on a printed menu given to a customer for selection of menu items. As shown in the

MENU ITEM	TALLY OF COLLECTION	TOTAL
Orange Juice	ЖЖ ЖЖ ЖЖ ЖЖ ЖЖ ЖЖ ЖЖ III	38
Grapefruit Juice	ЖЖ ЖЖ ЖЖ IIII	19
Honeydew Melon	ЖЖ ЖЖ ЖЖ ЖЖ ЖЖ	25
Scrambled Eggs (2)	ЖЖ ЖЖ ЖЖ ЖЖ II	22
Scrambled Eggs (1)	ЖЖ ЖЖ ЖЖ ЖЖ ЖЖ ЖЖ II	32
Poached Eggs (2)	ЖЖ ЖЖ ЖЖ	15
Fried Eggs (1)	ЖЖ ЖЖ ЖЖ ЖЖ II	22
Fried Eggs (2)	ЖЖ ЖЖ ЖЖ ЖЖ III	23
Hash Browns	ЖЖ ЖЖ ЖЖ III	18
Grits	ЖЖ ЖЖ ЖЖ ЖЖ ЖЖ I	26

Figure 2.3   Tally of breakfast menu item selections.

excerpt from a printed menu in Figure 2.3, the number of servings are recorded followed by the total number for a specific meal, in this case a breakfast.

A tabulation of each menu item demand for the same day, week, or meal should be recorded for forecasting purposes as shown in Table 2.8. To record data over time, a manual record book, index card system, or other system can be used. If the foodservice uses computer-assisted methods of data tabulation, the menu item demand can be organized and sorted by menu item, day of the week, or meal for the forecasting database. See Chapter 6 for the discussion of computer-assisted methods.

The menu selection combination is the varying factor. If scrambled eggs were served with the popular item of pancakes instead of fried eggs, the menu item demand would be different than that in Table 2.8. The selection of scrambled eggs changes with the popularity of the competing items. When scrambled eggs are competing with pancakes (see Table 2.9), an average of 21 percent of the customers selected eggs but when competing with French toast, 43 percent chose scrambled eggs. Each time choices are changed,

Table 2.8 Menu Item Demand Data by Rotation, Date, and Day

Date	Day	Menu Item	Menu Item Demand (Percent)
Rotation			
July 14	Mon	Fried Egg (1)	31
July 21	Mon	Fried Egg (1)	25
July 28	Mon	Fried Egg (1)	28
Rotation			
July 14	Mon	Scrambled Egg (1)	45
July 21	Mon	Scrambled Egg (1)	60
July 28	Mon	Scrambled Egg (1)	68

Table 2.9 Customer Selection (Percent) of Menu Item by Day

Item	Day 1	Day 8	Day 15	Average
Scrambled Eggs	20	33	27	21
Pancakes	80	67	73	79
	Day 4	Day 11	Day 18	Average
Scrambled Eggs	40	45	43	43
French Toast	60	55	57	57

menu item demand should be recorded and used for fore-casting. If a computer is available, menu item data can be easily sorted and stored. If a manual system is used, however, record keeping is more time consuming. The date, meal, and menu cycle rotation should be well-documented for database development. A mean of menu item data should be calculated for three or more observations before using the data in the forecast.

Restaurants and other foodservices that have tabulating cash registers can use the recorded menu items to obtain the menu item and customer demands. Some registers or hand held computer systems are pre-coded for each menu item. Therefore, the cashier becomes a key person in the collection of forecasting data.

If a production worksheet has an accurate volume to prepare and number of expected servings for each menu item, it becomes a major source document. The production worksheet, however, needs careful monitoring; production employees are busy and frequently forget to weigh or record the amounts of food items prepared or customer demand. Whatever the system, menu tally, cash register, waitperson's ticket, or production worksheets, accuracy must be maintained to provide good forecasting or other operational data.

Organizing Production Data

Data records, as shown in Tables 2.6 and 2.7, are samples of data sorting by like day and menu items in the menu cycle. This can be done for all major menu items to provide information to the forecaster.

Another method of evaluating demand is to plot data on a graph providing the forecaster and forecasting team a visual review of the data pattern. As an example, using the holiday data (300, 330, 350, 350, 380, 475, 460, 475) of pancakes in Table 2.7, a graph in an easy-to-read pattern, illustrates a demand increase over the eight-year period (Figure 2.4).

The number of customers ordering a ham and egg sandwich each day of the week are graphically displayed in Figure 2.5. This type of graph shows not only the variation in the number of customers selecting the sandwich each day of the week, but also emphasizes the volume increase on weekends.

COLLECTING DATA

Two types of data are important in forecasting menu items: (1) customer demand or census and (2) menu item demand. A forecast will generate the total number of expected customers or census.

Customer Demand Data

Customer demand data are the total number of customers who have eaten a meal. These customer demand data can be collected from a number of records depending on the foodservice operation. For instance, a restaurant may collect these data at the point-of-sale transaction, from guest checks or from host/hostess record of guest numbers.

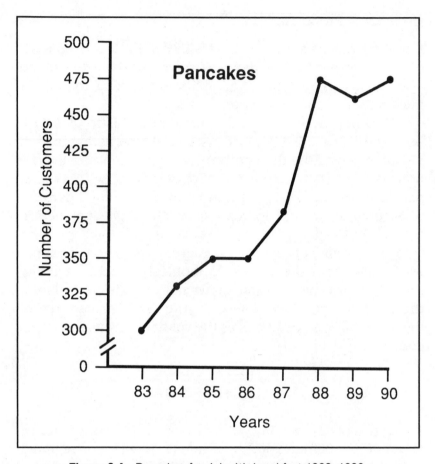

Figure 2.4 Pancakes for July 4th breakfast 1983–1990.

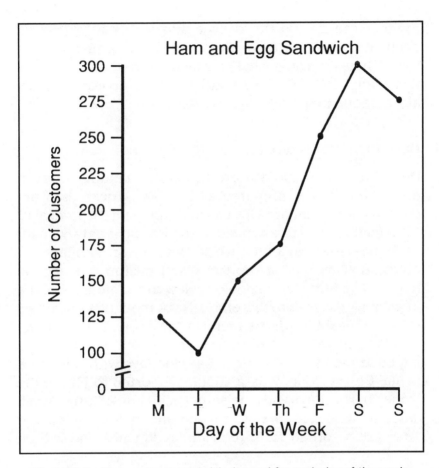

Figure 2.5 Ham and egg sandwich demand for each day of the week.

Another example is the college and university customer count at entry to the foodservice or at point-of-sale transaction. A hospital will collect census data from customer/patient completed menus, cafeteria sales, or records of covers at a catering event.

Menu Item Demand Data

Menu item demand data are the actual number of each menu item that is prepared and served. These data are collected and tabulated for use in developing the forecast.

Menu item data are needed to develop a database for each meal and day of the week. Data reflect similar variables such as day of the week and customer selection trends. The forecaster should review the same days of the week or like days and, therefore, the number of menu items sold will be similar if the menu is the same. For example, Monday generally has the same percentage of people eating each menu item as on other Mondays with the same menu. So, all Monday data should be sorted together, the same for Tuesdays with the same menu and all other week days. In Table 2.10, menu item demand for French Dip and Taco are recorded for three Monday lunches and will be

Table 2.10 Weekday Menu Item Demand

Date	Day	Meal	Menu Item	Menu Item Demand (Servings)
July 06	Mon	Lunch	French Dip	90
July 13	Mon	Lunch	French Dip	85
July 20	Mon	Lunch	French Dip	93
July 06	Mon	Lunch	Tacos	110
July 13	Mon	Lunch	Tacos	115
July 20	Mon	Lunch	Tacos	110

Table 2.11 Weekend Menu Item Demand

Date	Day	Meal	Menu Item	Menu Item Demand (Servings)
July 11	Sat	Dinner	Prime Rib	58
July 18	Sat	Dinner	Prime Rib	45
July 25	Sat	Dinner	Prime Rib	49
July 11	Sat	Dinner	Baked Sole	35
July 18	Sat	Dinner	Baked Sole	25
July 25	Sat	Dinner	Baked Sole	32

used to forecast the next Monday demands. Weekend data is much different than midweek data in restaurants, hospitals, schools, or any foodservice. Therefore, Saturday data should be tabulated or sorted together with other Saturday data. An example of menu item demand for Prime Rib and Baked Sole on the Saturday dinner menu is given in Table 2.11. The same logic applies in sorting holiday data as illustrated in Table 2.12. The customer has a choice of turkey or ham for Thanksgiving dinner from 1989 through 1991.

Table 2.12 Holiday (Thanksgiving) Menu Item Demand

Date	Day	Meal	Menu Item	Menu Item Demand (Servings)
Nov. 23, 1989	Thur	Dinner	Turkey	150
Nov. 22, 1990	Thur	Dinner	Turkey	163
Nov. 28, 1991	Thur	Dinner	Turkey	142
Nov. 23, 1989	Thur	Dinner	Ham	64
Nov. 22, 1990	Thur	Dinner	Ham	73
Nov. 28, 1991	Thur	Dinner	Ham	70

Another variable to be concerned with is the influence of competing food items on menu item demand. For example, when fried chicken and lasagna were on the menu for June 18, 46 percent of the customers chose the chicken (Table 2.13). On June 29, however, 73 percent of the customers chose fried chicken instead of pasta salad. if competing menu items have no effect on the percentage of customers selecting the popular fried chicken, then ongoing data collection would not be necessary for either purchasing or production forecasting.

Menu Tally System

Hospital foodservices often use complex tally systems to determine the amount of food to purchase and produce. Patients select the menu items they want for a meal. A clerk then records the number of servings selected for each menu item on a master tally sheet.

Forecasting will *eliminate* the need for a tally process before each meal. Tallying of menu items on a cycle menu is not necessary on a regular basis if a forecasting method has been implemented; however, past tallies serve as the database for developing the method. A tally would be used at random to check the forecast accuracy. Forecasts may be generated mathematically by using recorded data as explained in Chapter 3. Food items are often cooked before tallying is completed. Therefore, the amount of food items

Table 2.13 Influence of Competing Menu Items on Demand Data

| Date | Menu Item | Alternate Selection | Customers Selecting Chicken (Percent) | | | |
| | | | Observations | | | |
			1	2	3	Average
June 18	Fried Chicken	Lasagna	46	50	42	46
June 29	Fried Chicken	Pasta Salad	73	68	64	68

produced is actually determined by forecasting. For special orders, however, some type of tallying system is essential. Personnel formerly used for the tally process can be trained for the forecasting method.

DATA PATTERNS

A graphic display of data generally takes on a constant, trend, or seasonal pattern over time. A *constant* (horizontal) pattern shows very little change in the demand numbers. A constant demand may occur when there is no menu choice and each customer receives the same menu item or when the number of customers is nearly the same each day. An example would be where all the children in a summer

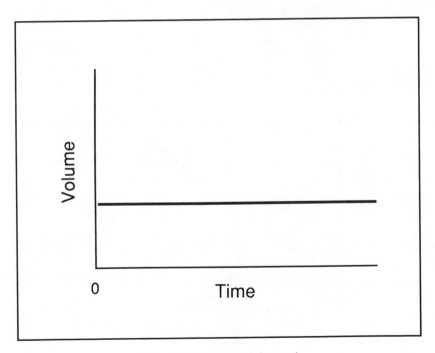

Figure 2.6   Constant demand.

camp receive a glass of milk with each meal. The milk usage would be nearly the same for each meal. (Figure 2.6). The *trend* demand pattern shows either a gradual increase or decrease in the data (Figure 2.7). In Table 2.7 and Figure 2.4, an increasing trend in pancake demand over the years is indicated in the July 4th data. A decreasing trend may result when a menu item is no longer popular or when a customer service is no longer available. For example, a factory closed nearby or traffic rerouted to another street, thus decreasing customer numbers. This trend could be gradual or sudden, requiring forecasts to be adjusted. A *seasonal* pattern (Figure 2.8) reflects a repeating pattern within the data. An example would be the increase of customers in a ski resort restaurant in the winter. In the reverse situation, a decrease in hospital pattern census occurs in December.

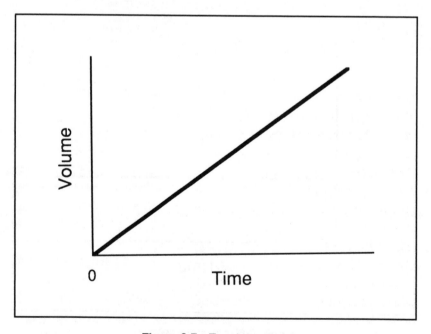

Figure 2.7 Trend demand.

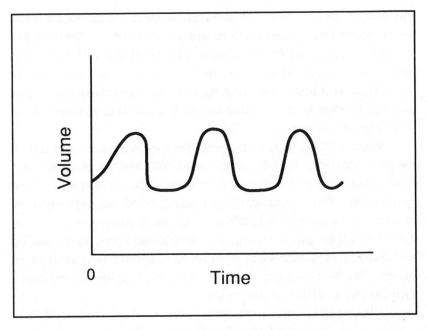

Figure 2.8 Seasonal demand.

WRAP UP

A review of records in the foodservice industry is an on-going task. The review is critical to assure the forecasting personnel that the data records are accurate. The major records to review for accurate data that will be used in forecasting are the menu, production worksheets/schedules, and recipes. The *menu* will be structured to offer the customer a single choice or multiple choice of menu items. The number of customers choosing each menu item is the menu item demand used as the basis for menu item forecasting. The *production worksheets/schedules* should contain the estimated amount of each menu item to produce, which is equivalent to the estimated forecast for each menu item. It also should have a record of how much of each menu item was used—the actual menu item demand. The difference of the estimated forecast and the actual should be recorded; this is known as the forecast error. *Recipes* are records that contain the amount of each ingredient that is used to produce the menu item. The use of an accurate recipe in which the yield or volume is standardized allows the head cook to adjust the volume of the recipe to produce the forecast amount.

Forecasting personnel are the foodservice forecaster, data recorder, head cook, and foodservice manager. The forecasting role should be identified for each of these personnel. The updated forecasting method may require modified or new job routines. An additional person may be needed to plan, train, and implement the forecasting method. However, with evaluation and reassignment of tasks, the forecasting method can be implemented without hiring additional personnel.

Production information is to be identified that will provide forecasting data. The decision on what to forecast is the first information needed. This decision will generally be customer count and the number of menu items sold per meal. A database is compiled by tabulating the demand for each menu item per meal. The popularity of each menu item in comparison with the competing menu items for each meal should be calculated. This data can be documented by popularity percentage and is useful in the forecasting method. The forecasting data that is important to the foodservice organization can be organized by sorting the data by like day and menu items in the menu cycle.

Collecting data of customer demand and menu item demand are critical to generate a good forecast. The customer demand is the total number of customers at each meal. Menu item demand data are the actual number of each item that is prepared and served. These data are collected and tabulated for use in developing the forecast. A menu tally system that is used in hospital foodservices can be eliminated once a forecasting method is implemented. However, special orders, items requested that are not on the menu, will still need to be recorded or tallied.

Data patterns appear in the documentation of record values for customer demand. The method to document and visually review the data are to plot the customer demand on a graph. The data will generally follow one of three patterns: (1) constant, (2) trend, or (3) seasonal. As a result of the plotting and review, a forecast method can be selected to accommodate the pattern.

ACTION

The foodservice manager and forecasting team should decide the items they wish to forecast. From this decision, data review will take on greater meaning. The following steps may be used:

1. Decide the forecast focus: customer demand, menu item demand, or both.
2. Identify the records that will be used to provide forecasting data.
3. Review method and accuracy of the following documents as they affect the forecast: Menu, production worksheets, and recipes.
4. Determine which personnel are currently involved in the forecasting function. Re-evaluate the role of key production and service personnel in implementing a new forecasting method.
5. Build a database of the needed data identified in step 1. This may include: (1) customer or census count and (2) menu item choices for each meal and day of the week. A minimum of three observations for each meal and day of the week having the same menu will probably be required.

6. Review data patterns of customer count or census for total number for each meal and days of the week and holidays.

REFERENCES

Adam, Jr., E. E., and Ebert, R. J., Production and Operations Management (4th ed.) (Englewood Cliffs, NJ: Prentice-Hall, 1989).

Shugart, G., and Molt, N., *Food for Fifty* (8th ed.) (New York: Macmillan, 1989).

Spears, M. C., *Foodservice Organization: A Managerial and Systems Approach* (New York: Macmillan, 1991).

West, B. B., Wood L. W., Harger, V., Shugart, G. S., and Payne-Palacio, J., *Foodservice in Institutions* (6th ed.) (New York: Macmillan, 1988).

Wheelwright, S. C., and Makridakis, S., *Forecasting Methods for Management* (4th ed.) (New York: John Wiley, 1985).

3

FORECASTING METHODS

F oodservice forecasting is a method used to estimate the number of customers anticipated for a meal period and their menu item choices. This projected information is used to plan the food production in foodservices. The methods of forecasting that will be included in this chapter use models, which are mathematical expressions using past or historical data, to calculate an average of past customer and menu item demands. The forecasting models and methods to be illustrated have been studied, tested, and recommended for use in foodservice. The moving average model and variations of the exponential smoothing models are most appropriate for effectiveness, simplicity, and cost of generating accurate forecasts. These two models are classified as *time series* models that are based on the assumption that actual occurrences follow an identifiable trend over time. To make past data useful, variations need to be reduced to a trend line that can be extended into the future. This procedure is known as *smoothing the data.* Time series models are the most suitable for short-term forecasts in foodservice operations.

Forecasting models will be discussed for manual implementation into the foodservice. Computer-assisted methods are discussed in Chapter 6. Once a forecasting method is developed for the foodservice, it can easily be adapted for computer usage. Recommended models are based on the knowledge that the number of customers in foodservice are different for each day of the week unless data analysis indicates otherwise. Forecasts, therefore, are generated for periods or intervals of seven days into the future, for example, Monday to Monday, Tuesday to Tuesday. The period of time into the future for which the forecast is made is identified as *lead time.* Using the same day of the week in the past to generate a forecast for the corresponding day, a lead time of 7, 14, or 21 days is recommended. The time series concept, illustrated in Figure 3.1, shows that past data for Mondays

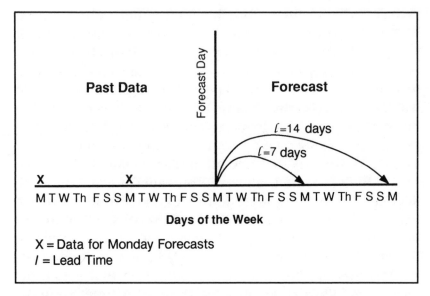

Figure 3.1 Time series model using past data to generate forecasts: Lead times of 7 and 14 days.

are used to forecast customer demand for subsequent Mondays with either a 7- or 14-day lead time.

The moving average or exponential smoothing forecasting models are recommended for use in foodservice. These quantitative models are effective in reducing the forecast error, thus controlling production costs.

MOVING AVERAGE MODEL

The moving average model is the easiest to use of the smoothing procedures. The first point on a trend line, as discussed in Chapter 2, is the average of a group of data. The second point is made by dropping the oldest data and adding the most recent before taking another average. The forecaster determines the amount of past demand data to include in the average, considering the fluctuations or randomness of the data. Generally, 4 to 10 past values of a like day of the week are used. Each week, the oldest demand number is dropped and the most recent is added. The average then becomes the forecast value for the succeeding Monday and indicates a trend. An example of the moving average forecasts for three subsequent Mondays is shown in Table 3.1 (p. 58).

In the example in Table 3.1, customer demand data for ten observations were used for the August 13 forecast. The sum of the customer demand data was divided by ten observations to produce the forecast of 683. The oldest value, 680, on June 4th was dropped the following day and the newest value, 698, on August 13th was added to generate the forecast of 684. Dropping the oldest value permits the most recent demand data to be used. The following tabulation shows the forecasts generated for the three dates in Table 3.1:

Forecasts	Dates
683	Aug. 13
684	Aug. 20
688	Aug. 27

Note the upward trend of the forecasts. This method is readily compatible with machine usage, such as a calculator or computer. Application of the moving average model is illustrated in Figure 3.2 (p. 59).

SIMPLE EXPONENTIAL SMOOTHING

Simple exponential smoothing models appear complex but are really very easy or "simple" to use. This forecasting

Table 3.1 Moving Average Model Using Ten Data
Observations for Customer Demand

Date (Mon)	Customer Demand		
	Data to Forecast Aug 13	Data to Forecast Aug 20	Data to Forecast Aug 27
June 04	680	—	—
June 11	672	672	—
June 18	683	683	683
June 25	689	689	689
July 02	678	678	678
July 09	690	690	690
July 16	697	697	697
July 23	687	687	687
July 30	679	679	679
Aug 06	671	671	671
Aug 13	—	698	698
Aug 20	—	—	712
Aug 27	—	—	—

Moving Average Model

$$F = \frac{\sum\limits_{i=1}^{N} D_i}{N}$$

In which

F = FORECAST
Σ = Summation
i = Unit of forecast (from 1 to number of Observations)
N = Number of Observations
D = Demand data (customer)

The formula can be illustrated for the August 13 forecast with data in Table 3.1 in which i equals Mondays and N equals 10 Observations.

Forecast = $\dfrac{680+672+683+689+678+690+697+687+679+671}{10}$ = 683

Figure 3.2 Illustration of use of moving average formula for generating a forecast for August 13th from past customer demand data.

model is different from the moving average model because it uses both the forecast value and customer demand data from the same day. The exponential smoothing component of the model is identified as the judgment factor because it requires the foodservice forecaster's professional judgment. This judgment factor known as the smoothing coefficient, alpha, indicates how well the forecaster believes the past data represent current customer count in the foodservice. Alpha, or judgment smoothing coefficient, is a number between 0 and 1 and is used to smooth randomness in the data. The number 1 is divided into two decimal parts, for example, alpha equals 0.3 and 1 minus alpha equals 0.7 or alpha equals 0.2 and 1 minus alpha equals 0.8.

If the last forecast differed greatly from the normal data due to some unforeseen circumstance, such as a snowstorm, these data would not be representative. Therefore, greater reliance should be placed on the recent forecast value for that snowy day than on the normal customer demand data when preparing the new forecast.

The judgment value is divided to provide a percentage or weight on both the demand and forecast values to generate the next forecast. In Table 3.2, the rationale for selecting the judgment smoothing coefficient, alpha, for demand data and the remainder, 1 minus alpha, for forecast data is given.

The value of alpha, the judgment factor or smoothing coefficient, has been tested in foodservice. If no major changes occur in the data, the customer demand for the succeeding weeks is not expected to differ greatly from the past, in which case, an alpha of 0.3 is commonly used for demand leaving 0.7 for the weight of the forecast. The last customer demand is multiplied by 0.3, alpha, and the last forecast by 0.7, 1 minus alpha. In the cited example of a snowstorm, the judgment factor may be changed to 0.1 for customer demand, thus weighting the last forecast 0.9 $(1 - 0.1)$.

Table 3.2 Rationale for Selection of the Judgment
Smoothing Coefficient, Alpha, for Demand Data

Demand (alpha)*	Forecast (1 – alpha)	Rationale
0.1	0.9	Forecast data more reliable than demand data.
0.2	0.8	
0.3	0.7	
0.4	0.6	
0.5	0.5	Equal weight on demand and forecast data.
0.6	0.4	
0.7	0.3	
0.8	0.2	
0.9	0.1	Demand data more reliable than forecast data.

* Judgment smoothing coefficient

The model in Figure 3.3 is used to compute the new
customer demand forecast for the next production period.
The new forecast is for August 13th and it is computed from
the customer demand and forecast data of August 6th. The
exponential smoothing model in mathematical formulation
is shown in Figure 3.4. An example of mathematical calculations for the simple exponential smoothing model is displayed in Figure 3.5.

For example:

$$8/13 \text{ Forecast} = \left(\begin{matrix} \text{Judgment} \\ \text{Factor} \end{matrix}\right) \left(8/16 \begin{matrix} \text{Customer} \\ \text{Demand} \end{matrix}\right)$$
$$+ \left(1 - \begin{matrix} \text{Judgment} \\ \text{Factor} \end{matrix}\right) \left(8/16 \text{ Forecast}\right)$$

Figure 3.3 Simple exponential smoothing model expressed in words with
example.

$$F_{t+1} = \alpha D_t + (1 - \alpha) F_t$$

Where:

F   = Forecast
t   = Time
t + 1 = Forecast Date (Time plus One Period into the Future)
α   = Judgment Factor (Alpha Coefficient)
D   = Customer Demand

Figure 3.4   Simple exponential smoothing formulation.

$$\text{Forecast}_{(\text{Date}+1)} = \left(\begin{array}{c}\text{Judgment}\\\text{Factor}\end{array}\right)\left(\begin{array}{c}\text{Customer}\\\text{Demand}\\_{(\text{Date})}\end{array}\right) + \left(1 - \begin{array}{c}\text{Judgment}\\\text{Factor}\end{array}\right)\left(\begin{array}{c}\text{Forecast}\\_{(\text{Date})}\end{array}\right)$$

June 3 Mon	=	(.3)	$\left(\dfrac{500}{5/27}\right)$	+	(.7)	$\left(\dfrac{515}{5/27}\right)$	=	511
June 10 Mon	=	(.3)	$\left(\dfrac{510}{6/3}\right)$	+	(.7)	$\left(\dfrac{511}{6/13}\right)$	=	511
June 17 Mon	=	(.1)	$\left(\dfrac{525}{6/10}\right)$	+	(.9)	$\left(\dfrac{511}{6/10}\right)$	=	513
June 24 Mon	=	(.2)	$\left(\dfrac{512}{6/17}\right)$	+	(.8)	$\left(\dfrac{513}{6/17}\right)$	=	513
July 1 Mon	=	(.3)	$\left(\dfrac{515}{6/24}\right)$	+	(.7)	$\left(\dfrac{513}{6/24}\right)$	=	514

Figure 3.5   Simple exponential smoothing model for computing a new forecast using past customer demand and forecast data over time.

The forecaster may want to plot the demand data and the forecast to compare the accuracy of the forecast. This display aids the forecaster in judging the accuracy of the forecast by comparison to the customer demand data pattern (see Figure 3.6). Data in week three had an unusually high customer demand. The high customer demand was unusual and therefore a smaller 0.1 judgment factor was placed on the data for June 17 and a 0.2 judgment factor on the demand for June 24 to minimize the effect that the high customer demand would have in calculating the new forecast for June 24 and July 1. In using the data for a new forecast, the forecast for Week 4 will be more typical. In using the simple exponential smoothing model, therefore, greater weight would be placed on the forecast

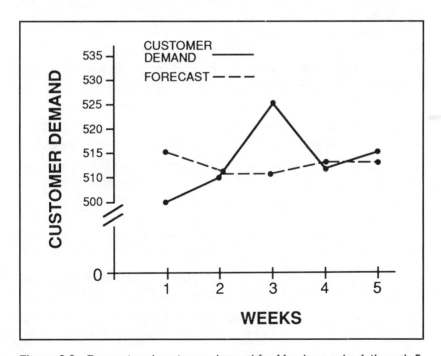

Figure 3.6 Forecast and customer demand for Monday weeks 1 through 5, using data from Figure 3.5.

than on the customer demand, as discussed in the snow-storm example. This simple exponential smoothing model "smoothes" out the randomness of the customer demand data in Week 4 when the new forecast is computed.

Rationale for the Simple Exponential Smoothing Model

The simple exponential smoothing model is designed to eliminate storage of historical records because all past data are considered in the smoothing process over time for a new forecast. This is due to the judgment factor that enables a part of the history as well as current demand values to be represented in the computation of the new forecast. Consequently, the numerous past records do not need to be saved for generating a forecast.

Exponential smoothing derives its name from the use of the judgment factor, which purports to reduce errors, by smoothing out the variation in past demand and forecast values. This technique prevents unusual customer demands from heavily influencing the next forecast. For this reason, exponential smoothing has been shown to be very effective for foodservice. In addition, it is easy to use and inexpensive for lead time or periods of 7-day intervals into the future, for example 7-, 14-, 21-, or 28-day lead times.

Data Formulation for Simple Exponential Smoothing Model

The forecasting procedure is designed for a future period of time. Generally, this will be for the next week's food production, seven days away. To implement the forecast model, the following steps have been identified for generating a forecast for customer demand.

Step 1 Identify the date of the new forecast.

Step 2 Locate the past customer demand and the forecast of customer demand from historical data of the same day of the week. These values may be on the production worksheet or tabulated on a separate data record. *Note:* If past records (new restaurant or lost records) are not available, a past customer demand and forecast value must be estimated in order to start the formula.

Step 3 Determine the judgment factor. The recommended starting values are 0.3 for customer demand and 0.7 (1 – judgment factor) for the forecast.

Step 4 Insert the *demand, forecast,* and *judgment factor* values into the simple exponential smoothing formula.

Step 5 Complete the mathematical computation by multiplying the customer demand by the judgment factor and the forecast by 1 minus the judgment factor.

Step 6 Round the computed new forecast to a whole number. The result of the computation is the forecast for a specific date.

As illustrated in Figure 3.5, the computed forecast becomes the last forecast in the next computation. Keeping track of dates of the new forecast and past customers demands and forecast is quite important. Actual customer demand and the forecast for the same day are retrieved from production worksheets or other data sources.

ADAPTIVE EXPONENTIAL SMOOTHING

As the forecaster becomes more familiar with the simple exponential smoothing technique and the database, some model changes can be made. Simple exponential smoothing uses a judgment factor for each set of data. The adaptive exponential model uses a nonfixed judgment factor to adapt to changes in the data.

The adaptive exponential smoothing model is most effective if it is computer-assisted. The computer is used to change automatically the judgment factor to adapt to the data change. A tracking signal, a computer-assisted technique, can be used. This tracking signal, which is calculated by dividing smoothed error by smoothed absolute error, was developed by Trigg and Leach[*] to calculate automatically a new judgment factor, based on the difference of the forecast and actual demand. In the adaptive exponential smoothing model, the tracking signal value is generated automatically, as each forecasting error becomes available and replaces the judgment factor in the exponential smoothing model.

BOX-JENKINS

Box and Jenkins developed a forecasting technique that integrates auto-regressive and moving average techniques to obtain estimates of demand values. Practical application of the Box-Jenkins model involves an iterative computer process and is very complex. This model works very well in generating a customer demand forecast in foodservice as tested by Messersmith, Moore, and Hoover.[†] However, these models are more costly to use than the exponential smoothing model and require the assistance of a programming technician. For these reasons, the

---

[*] Trigg, D. W., and Leach, A. G., "Exponential smoothing with an adaptive response rate," *Operations Research Quarterly* 18:1:53, 1967.
[†] Messersmith, A. M., Moore, A. N., and Hoover, L. W., "A multi-echelon menu item forecasting system for hospitals," *Journal of the American Dietetic Association* 72:509, 1978.

model is *not* recommended unless sophisticated support systems are available. Simple and adaptive smoothing models have been shown by Messersmith to be about equally effective when used with lead times of 7, 14, or 21 days (multiples of 7 to assure like data).

MENU ITEM PREFERENCE STATISTIC

Menu item preference data combines customer demand and menu item demand. The forecasting model can be used to generate the forecast for customer demand or for menu item demand. However, instead of applying the exponential smoothing or moving average model to each menu item, a preference statistic can be calculated for menu item forecasting. *Customer demand forecast* is estimated by using data from customer count, census, or point-of-sale records. To generate the number of customers estimated for a future data. *Menu item forecast* can be estimated using a forecasting model with data from the menu item demand or number of portions for each item. This procedure requires extensive use of model data and can be more efficient with the use of a *preference statistic* that is calculated for each menu item. The preference statistic is used where two or more choices of a menu item within a category, such as soup or salad, are available. The number of customers selecting each choice are divided by the total number of customers to give the proportion or percentage of customers choosing each menu item.

Menu item frequency data can be collected by the data recorder from cash register records, menu item tallies or customer orders. A minimum of three observations of the same menu choices for the same meal and the same day of the week must be made. The proportion of customers selecting each menu item is then averaged giving a preference statistic for each choice in the category.

In Table 3.3, for example, the menu item, Chicken Bisque Soup, was selected on consecutive Thursdays by 6 percent of the customers on June 7, 10 percent on June 14, and 13 percent on June 21. The *average* of these three observations is 10 percent and becomes the preference statistic for forecasting Chicken Bisque Soup on this menu. The preference statistic may be used until the menu is changed or major changes in customer selections are observed and then the process needs to be repeated.

The forecasting model will generate an estimated number of customers. The menu item preference statistic, sometimes referred to as the popularity index or demand percentage, is applied to the estimated number of customers to determine the likely number to select a particular menu item. An example of the application for Chicken Bisque Soup (Table 3.3) is:

Customer demand forecast	518
Preference statistic	× 0.10
Number of customers	51.8 or 52

Therefore, 52 customers are estimated to select Chicken Bisque Soup.

This method of calculation can be done with each menu item. If the foodservice uses computer-assisted techniques, these data can be easily manipulated. If the calculations are done manually, a record can be kept.

WRAP UP

Foodservice forecasting is a method used to estimate the number of customers anticipated for a meal period and their menu item choices. The technique used to generate forecasts uses customer demand and menu item demand of the past data. Foodservice has similar data corresponding with

Table 3.3 Menu Item Choices by Category for Three Identical Thursday Menus with Proportion of Customers and Preference Statistic for Each Choice

Category: Menu Item Choices	Observation Dates			Preference Statistic*
	6-7-90 (Thur)	6-14-90 (Thur)	6-21-90 (Thur)	
	-------- Proportion of Customers --------			
Soup or Salad				
Chicken Bisque Soup	.06	.10	.13	.10
Beef Barley Soup	.10	.15	.08	.11
Green Salad	.80	.71	.79	.77
None	.04	.04	0	.02
Entree				
Salmon Steak	.30	.35	.28	.31
Rib Eye Steak	.52	.45	.46	.48
Pork Loin Chops	.17	.20	.25	.21
None	.01	0	.01	0
Vegetable				
Asparagus Spears	.50	.45	.55	.50
Green Beans Almandine	.31	.38	.26	.32
Broiled Tomatoes	.19	.17	.19	.18
None	0	0	0	0

* Preference statistic: Average proportion of customers for three observations.

days of the week, thus, are intervals of 7-days. It is suggested to forecast into the future for 7, 14, or 21 days, as the accuracy will be more dependable than other time intervals.

Two models are recommended for forecasting foodservice customer demand: (1) moving average and (2) simple exponential smoothing. Others that can be used are adaptive exponential smoothing and Box-Jenkins. These models are more complex and usually more expensive but results have been shown to be similar to moving average or exponential smoothing.

Combining customer demand and menu item demand into a forecasting method provides the total expected number of customers and the demand of each major menu item. The forecasting model is used to generate customer demand, and the preference statistic is computed to determine the percentage of customers choosing each menu item. To utilize these techniques, historical data are collected in a minimum of three observations of each menu item. A preference statistic value can be calculated for use in the forecasting technique. The more accurate the data, the better the forecast.

ACTION

The forecasting team will determine which model to use for the forecasting method to be developed. The action is as follows:

1. Test the forecasting models.
2. Select the most appropriate forecasting model.
3. Review data source documents for
   (a) Forecasts
   (b) Customer demand
   (c) Menu item demand.

4. Formulate data in source documents for easy tabulation.

5. Develop database for

   (a) Customer demand

   (b) Menu item proportions (menu item preference statistic).

6. Determine customer demand pattern through graphic display.

REFERENCES

Adam, E. A., and Ebert, R. J., *Production and Operations Management* (4th ed.) (Englewood Cliffs, N.J: Prentice-Hall, 1989).

Box, G. E. P., and Jenkins, G. M., *Time Series Analysis Forecasting and Control* (San Francisco: Holden-Day, 1970).

Messersmith, A. M., Moore, A. N., and Hoover, L. W., "A multiechelon menu item forecasting system for hospitals," *Journal of the American Dietetic Association* 72:509, 1978.

Miller, J. L., and Shanklin, C. S., "Forecasting menu item demand in foodservice operations," *Journal of the American Dietetic Association* 88:4:443, 1988.

Spears, M. C., *Foodservice Organizations: A Managerial and Systems Approach* (2d ed.) (New York: Macmillan, 1991).

Trigg, D. W., and Leach, A. G., "Exponential smoothing with an adaptive response rate," *Operations Research Quarterly* 18:1:53, 1967.

Wheelwright, S. C., and Makridakis, S., *Forecasting Methods for Management,* (4th ed.) (New York: John Wiley, 1985).

4

EVALUATING THE
FORECASTING METHOD

valuation is a procedure that "fine tunes" the forecasting method to assure accuracy and reliability. The closer the forecast is to actual demand, the more accurate and reliable is the forecast. The difference between a forecast and actual customer or menu item demand is identified as the *forecast error*. In Table 4.1, a forecast error record is shown; the forecast error for each of ten observations equals the forecast minus the actual demand. Over-or under-production increases costs. Efficient foodservice managers, therefore, are eager to keep the error small with the concomitant result of controlling costs. Evaluation of the magnitude of the error becomes imperative in the selection of a forecasting model. After the model goes through the test stage, it must go through the operational stage before final selection.

TEST STAGE

In the test stage, data from records prior to adoption of a forecasting model need to be examined to determine if the amount of food prepared was too much, just right, or too little. The difference between the amount prepared

Table 4.1 Forecast Error Record

Observation	Forecast[a]	Actual Demand	Forecast Error[b]
1	310	300	10
2	307	310	−3
3	308	295	13
4	304	304	0
5	304	298	6
6	302	300	2
7	301	315	−14
8	305	302	3
9	304	299	5
10	303	305	−2

[a] Forecast of customer or menu item demand.
[b] Forecast Error = Forecast − Actual Demand.

of specific items on the menu and the customer count or menu item demand, which really is a forecast error, should be noted. After a model is selected, the same menu should be repeated and the same data collected; the difference between the new forecast and customer or menu item demand becomes the forecast error.

The forecaster then compares the error before and after the use of the model to ascertain any changes or improvements. If the forecasting model error is less than before, the decision usually is made to adopt it. If, however, the error is greater than before, the model might need to be modified or another model selected. If the exponential smoothing model was used, changing the judgment factor might give a more accurate forecast.

OPERATIONAL STAGE

The selected forecasting model becomes operational when it is used over time and the results are accepted by management. As in any decision-making situation, an evaluation component is required before acceptance of a decision. Error measurement is a reliable means for evaluating a forecasting model and should be done each time the model is used. To evaluate forecasts over time, any one of or a combination of three popular error measurements can be used: Bias, Mean Absolute Deviation (MAD), and Mean Square Error (MSE).

Bias

The average of the errors in the forecast model, taking into account the sign of each, is identified as the bias of the forecast. A positive bias implies that the forecast gives estimates that are too high; a negative bias too low. As shown

Table 4.2 Evaluation of Errors Using Bias, Mean Absolute
Deviation (MAD), and Mean Square Error (MSE) Measures

Observation	Bias	MAD	MSE
1	10	10	100
2	−3	3	9
3	13	13	169
4	0	0	0
5	6	6	36
6	2	2	4
7	−14	14	196
8	3	3	9
9	5	5	25
10	−2	2	4
Sum of Errors	20	58	552
Average Errors	2	5.8	55.2

in the Bias column of Table 4.2, the sum of the errors of measurement is divided by the number of observations to give the bias of the forecasts: $+20 \div 10 = +2$. Three forecast errors, 10, 13, and -14, are greater than the others and should be reviewed.

Evaluation of forecasting errors for ten observations gives an average of +2 errors for that period indicating over-forecasting two customers or menu items. Most food-service managers prefer this result because it does not cause immediate service problems. Leftover food can be stored or thrown out without disturbing production. Under-forecasting, indicated by a negative bias, however, causes immediate production problems. Employees become stressed because substitutions have to be made, and customers unhappy because their selection is not available and serving time might be delayed.

Forecasting models can be compared by using the same demand data and evaluating error measurements. The average error bias for the moving average and simple exponential smoothing models is shown in Table 4.3. The

Table 4.3   Comparison of Moving Average (MA) and
Simple Exponential Smoothing (SES) for Error Bias

Observations	MA Forecast Error	SES Forecast Error
1	4	10
2	−8	−3
3	7	13
4	−5	0
5	6	6
6	4	2
7	−13	−14
8	2	3
9	6	5
10	0	2
Sum of Errors	3	20
Average Error Bias	.3	+2

simple exponential smoothing model would probably be chosen by the forecaster because it has a +0.3 average error bias compared to a +2 for the moving average.

Mean Absolute Deviation (MAD)

MAD is designed to measure the average magnitude of forecasting errors by ignoring the positive and negative signs of the deviations from the mean and using absolute values as shown in the MAD column of Table 4.2. The sum of the errors of measurement is divided by the number of observations to give the mean absolute deviation: $58 \div 10 = 5.8$. MAD indicates to the forecaster the magnitude of the error but not over- or under-production errors as a result of the forecast. The forecaster should select a moving average or simple exponential smoothing forecasting method based on the lowest MAD and the lowest positive Bias.

Mean Square Error (MSE)

MSE is used as a measure of accuracy of the forecasting method. Absolute values of errors are squared before summing as shown in the MSE column of Table 4.2. The sum of errors is divided by the number of observations: $552 \div 10 = 55.2$ MSE penalizes a forecast that generates extremely large forecast errors more than one that generates small errors. MSE gives unbiased estimates of customer and menu item demands. This error measurement can be used alone or in conjunction with Bias or MAD.

ERROR MEASUREMENT SELECTION

The error measurements—bias, mean absolute deviation (MAD), and mean square error (MSE)—are methods by which the forecasting can be monitored. Each meal or day forecasts are documented as a forecast error (forecasts minus customer demand). After a number of forecasts (two weeks or more) are made, error measurements can be calculated for the series of forecast. These error measurements provide a method for the forecasting team to evaluate the forecasting model.

The forecasting team can select one or more of the error measurements to calculate the average magnitude of the forecasting errors over the series of forecasts. Forecasts ideally should equal the customer demand. If there are forecast errors, it is preferred that the error is small and positive. This small positive error allows for over-production rather than under-production. To determine the accuracy of the forecasting, one of the three error measurements can be used. Alternatively, you may want to use each method and compare the results.

For example, error measurement and outcome values in a medium sized foodservice with 350 customers could be:

Bias: An average of a small positive error such as (+)2 to (+)12 bias helps the forecaster to evaluate if the forecasting model is under- or over-forecasting.

MAD: An average of errors without indicating minus or positive forecast errors. An example of the error magnitude could be approximately 6 to 26. This measurement is used to determine the average size of all errors (negative and positive).

MSE: An average of the absolute errors squared provides a positive number. The greatest forecasting errors are penalized and a large number results. The average squared errors that are 55 or greater indicate that there are large forecasting errors.

It is advisable to select one or more error measurements. Bias is recommended to provide the average of positive and minus forecast errors if only one error measurement technique is used.

INTERPRETING ERROR MEASURES

The interpretation of error measurement values of bias, mean absolute deviation, and mean square error were discussed. Quite often, a visual or graphic presentation will clarify the interpretation. A major decision needs to be made by the forecast team members before an evaluation method can be chosen. "What is an acceptable error for the foodservice operation?" This decision is based on the operation philosophy. For example, is over-production desirable to prevent a shortage of menu items? Perhaps, the managers elect to never have over-production or leftover menu items; negative forecast errors, therefore, are very acceptable. After operational decisions are made regarding acceptable error levels, results may be visualized.

Tolerance limits for the forecast error can be recorded on a control chart for visual evaluation. Tolerance limits are control points with upper and lower bounds on a control chart to provide a record of forecast error acceptability. In fact, the management decision may be to reject a forecasting method that generates an error that is unacceptable. Control charts with tolerance limits can be used to plot the forecast error values and/or for the error measurement values. An example of a control chart for recording forecast errors or bias forecast error measurement is shown in Figure 4.1.

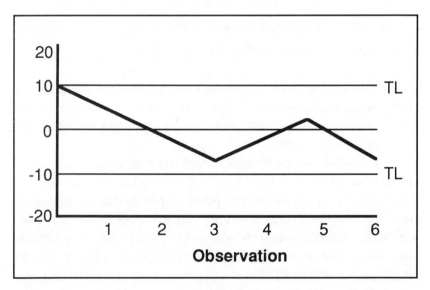

Figure 4.1 Control chart with tolerance limits for forecast error or bias error measurements.

A graphic presentation also permits the forecaster or forecast team to visually review the accuracy of the forecasting method. An inspection technique comparing forecast and demand data is shown in Figure 4.2. The two values, forecast (F) and demand (D) data are plotted on a graph showing the number of customers or menu item servings at several time observations.

Many data observations can be plotted on a graph, to provide a rapid review of the forecasting results. When the plotted values fall outside the tolerance limits in Figure 4.1, the forecasting method needs to be reviewed.

Corrective Action

Three major corrective actions can be taken when forecasts are considered unacceptable after evaluation:

1. Review forecast models
2. Adjust preference statistics
3. Revise production.

The forecasting team will need to review the *forecasting models* for correctness. Perhaps a change in the data pattern may have occurred and the forecasting models will need to be adjusted.

Preference statistics will need to be recalculated when menu changes have been made. Each menu change causes different menu items to compete within the menu cycle or perhaps the weather changed sooner than anticipated, which affects the customers' menu item choice. *Production data collection* needs to be revised if production methods are changed. Production procedures may vary with changes in personnel. Therefore, additional training of production personnel may be needed to emphasize the importance of

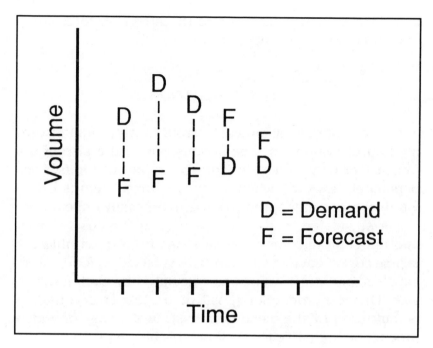

Figure 4.2   Graphic presentation of forecast (F) and demand (D) values.

using standardized recipes and the effect on forecasting and other operational procedures.

COST EVALUATION

A cost evaluation of forecast errors is a straightforward method of evaluation. The seriousness of the size of the forecast error is often difficult to explain to foodservice personnel. However, when a cost per menu item is calculated, over- or under-production is more easily understood.

A suggested method of calculating the cost of over- and under-production of menu items is to determine the selling cost of each menu item. This is based on food, labor, supplies, and profit values as calculated by each foodservice. The over-production (positive forecast error) quantity is multiplied by the menu item cost. In the case of under-production (negative forecast error), the cost is that of the replaced menu item or estimated cost of loss of goodwill. Also, supervisory personnel time for deciding a menu item substitution is a cost factor. Therefore, the negative error menu item costs generally are considered more expensive than positive errors or over-production.

The forecast error becomes a very meaningful value when a cost is associated with it. Many over-produced menu items can be refrigerated or frozen for future use, but handling and loss of food quality costs must be added. The cost of menu items is an operational decision. The decision may be to add a percentage of the menu item food cost to accommodate the handling cost of under- or over-production. Whatever the cost structure is, it needs to be consistent and easily calculated.

Each foodservice manager needs to make the appropriate decision for evaluating the cost of the substituted or leftover menu item. Table 4.4 provides an example of a forecast error cost record.

Table 4.4   Cost Record of Menu Item Forecast Error (FE)

Menu Item Cost	Forecast Error Negative[a]	Forecast Error Positive[b]	Cost per Portion Menu Item	Cost per Portion Handling[c]	Total FE Cost
BBQ Ribs		10	$5.00		$ 50.00
Roast Beef	−15		1.45		
(Pot Roast subst)			1.50	1.50	23.05
Baked Chicken	−6		1.70		
(Sliced Turkey subst)			1.85	1.50	9.90
Broiled Salmon		20	6.75		135.00
Total Cost of Forecast Error					$158.25

[a] Negative error costs were calculated by multiplying the sum of the menu item cost difference and handling costs for the substituted menu item by the number of items sold.
[b] Positive error costs were calculated by multiplying the cost per portion by the number of errors.
[c] Handling cost for negative errors.

WRAP UP

Evaluation "fine tunes" the forecasting method or model to assure accuracy and reliability. The closer the forecast is to the actual demand, the more accurate and reliable is the forecast. The forecasts can be monitored by evaluating the forecast error and respective costs in a test and operational stage.

A test stage uses past data to test the selected model and lead times for accuracy. If the forecast error is satisfactory, then accept the forecasting method. If not, continue to study and test different forecasting models.

The operational stage is when the selected forecasting model is implemented. There are three error measurements—bias, mean absolute deviation and mean square error—that can be used. These error measurements can measure the magnitude of forecast errors when forecasts are generated by any forecasting model. Forecasts that produce a minimum error when compared to the customer demand are most acceptable. The errors or error measurements can be graphically displayed for visual review. If unacceptable errors result, there is a need for corrective action. The forecasting method is to be reviewed, including forecasting model, preference data, production procedures, and lead times.

Cost evaluation of forecast error is a straightforward method of evaluation. A calculation of the cost of the under- and over-production of menu items as a result of forecasting error is recorded. The cost information is the menu item costs, menu item cost difference of substituted item and under- or over-forecasting error.

Action

An evaluation of the forecasting method designed for the foodservice production unit is to be completed. The following action plan is recommended:

1. Select the time period from the past to test the forecasting method using the forecast and customer demand data.
2. Test the forecasting method over the past data period, a minimum of four weeks of data is recommended.
   (a) Generate the forecast error.
   (b) Evaluate the forecast error using forecast error measurements.
3. Adjust the forecasting method to provide an acceptable forecast, forecast error and error measurements.
   (a) Record forecast errors and/or forecast error measurements on control charts.

(b) Plot demand data on a graph for additional visual evaluation.

4. Evaluate the test and operational stages with menu item and handling costs with the number of under- or over-forecasting of menu items.

5. Correct the forecasting method to provide acceptable forecasting results as needed, based on forecast error and cost evaluation.

(a) Adjust forecast model.

(b) Correct preference statistic.

(c) Review production operation techniques.

REFERENCES

Adam, E. E., and Ebert, R. J., *Production and Operations Management* (4th ed.) (Englewood Cliffs, N.J: Prentice-Hall, 1989).

Messersmith, A. M., Moore, A. N., and Hoover, L. W., "A multi-echelon menu item forecasting system for hospitals." *Journal of the American Dietetic Association 72:*509, 1978.

Wheelwright, S. C., and Makridakis, S., *Forecasting Methods for Management* (4th ed.) (New York: John Wiley, 1985).

5

PUTTING IT ALL TOGETHER

oodservice forecasting is a very important operational function that is often poorly understood. The forecasting methods detailed in this book serve as a guide to foodservice managers and forecasting team members. Using these concepts, foodservice managers will be able to discuss with administrators, owners, and other personnel the need for developing and implementing a forecasting method.

The major components of a foodservice forecasting method are presented with a detailed "walk through" approach including:

1. Forecasting and production methods review
2. Production records and database development
3. Forecast model description and development of menu item preference records
4. Forecast error evaluation.

The last chapter is designed to guide the forecaster through a computer-assisted method using a spreadsheet technique. In this chapter, some concepts will be presented that enhance the forecasting method implementation.

In foodservice, forecasting is used to estimate a wide range of activities or events that will affect the success of the operation. The estimate or forecast of the number of customers on a given day and meal is the major forecasting activity. The next important estimate is to project the menu item choices that the customers will select for their meal. The forecasts for these activities provides a database for decision making and planning in the foodservice. Forecasting is a technique that uses past information or data in a systematic way to estimate future needs. Therefore, forecasting in foodservice organizations is a function of production.

The objective of foodservice professionals is to have the foodservice organization provide food and service to customers at an affordable price. An affordable price varies by the type of foodservice and customer. A restaurant would determine a price that includes an acceptable profit margin; whereas, a not-for-profit school foodservice would price food within specified budgets. To be able to meet the objectives, production and service procedures must be in place and monitored. A contributory function of production and service is to forecast the number of customers and their menu item choices, in order to prepare correct amounts of menu items and have them available for service to the customer.

To have an effective forecasting function, the foodservice production unit must have quantity and quality standards of production. The production unit produces menu items for a particular time and cost, with records of each kept for evaluating and planning for future production.

THE NEED FOR A FORECASTING METHOD

Over-production is an indicator of a forecasting problem. Over-production is readily evident with excess menu items and higher food costs. The leftover food from over-production must be refrigerated, frozen, or discarded. Each of the three methods of handling the over-production is expensive. Refrigerated menu items lose quality, consume refrigerator space, and require replanning into a menu within a day or two. Frozen menu items also lose quality, require space, and replanning. However, the frozen menu items can remain in frozen storage for a few weeks if necessary. Higher food costs occur when the menu item cannot be stored at reduced temperatures for later use and must be discarded. Gelatin salads, cream pies, and vegetable or fruit salads with dressings are examples of leftover foods that cannot be planned for reuse and that break down in quality and therefore need to be discarded. Over-production for some vegetables and meats can be replanned into soups. Each menu item that is over-produced must be rehandled for storage or discard. The rehandling process consumes labor time, storage materials or containers, and refrigerator or freezer space. These costs could be avoided if the over-production had not occurred.

Under-production is another indicator of a forecasting problem. In this case, the customer is directly affected by not being able to select the scheduled menu item. Under-production must be managed by substituting a similar menu item or reducing the customer's choices by not providing a substituted item. An example of a substitute for Red Snapper could be Salmon Steak, but this is a more expensive substitute. Baked acorn squash could be substituted by frozen mashed squash. In the first example, the substitute of salmon was more expensive, in the second, mashed squash is a lesser cost and menu form. In each case, the customer will be disappointed and may have difficulty in making choices for the meal.

Customer satisfaction will be reduced if menu choices are not available due to under-production. An example could be when a customer selects the foodservice for the popular clam chowder and learns that the chowder is not available and the substitute soup is cream of mushroom. This customer may not return to the foodservice and loss of revenue will result. Over-production will cause the customer to be dissatisfied if the replanned menu item from the freezer is not as good as expected. For example, the loss of moisture in a reheating procedure for beef stew could make the stew dry and unacceptable. In each case of either over- or under-production, the loss of customers is likely and loss of revenue may follow.

Profit loss will be affected when over- and under-production occurs. Over-production requires additional labor to store the reusable menu item and loss of food when menu items are discarded. Under-production causes higher food costs and labor time to prepare substituted menu items. In each case, there is the likelihood of customer loss, thus, revenue loss.

Foodservice personnel attitudes may change when the forecasting and production amounts are very different. Extra work is required to accommodate over- and under-production. Attitude changes can be transferred to absence from the job and negative comments to other foodservice workers, friends, and family. The service persons who interact with customers may not present menu item changes with the positive attitude that can reduce customer support and a loss in revenue.

IMPLEMENTING CONCERNS

Implementation of a forecasting method takes time and effort. The steps of the forecasting process, described in previous chapters, are:

- Maintaining production and service records
- Collecting customer and menu item demands
- Selecting a forecasting model
- Testing the forecast method using past data
- Implementing the forecasting method
- Evaluating the forecasts and making adjustments.

In addition to the operation procedures, a conceptual plan needs to be presented to administrators, as well as a time schedule and costs of implementing the forecasting method. Personnel training, modification of production and service forms, and evaluation reporting need to be planned as well.

Conceptual Plan

A conceptual plan including expected time schedule, costs, and outcome needs to be developed for foodservice administrators, owners, or other controlling personnel. The purpose of such a plan is to gain understanding, support, and financial approval. The conceptual plan will need to provide a straightforward procedure to the controlling personnel who may not understand forecasting methods or the importance of the function. A *time schedule* would include time estimates for the implementing concerns that are addressed in this section as well as the forecasting method technical steps addressed throughout this book.

Implementation costs will vary according to the foodservice organization structure and depth of work needed to incorporate a forecasting system. Anticipated costs will be in the areas of personnel and supplies. Personnel may need to be reassigned, upgraded, and trained. In some organizations, an additional person may need to be hired temporarily to assist with the implementation procedures. Costs for supplies may include new production record documents, personnel training documents, and computer software if the foodservice is computer-assisted.

Personnel Training

Training is important for all personnel connected with the forecasting method. The training would include the basic need and explanation of forecasting as it relates to the overall organization and to each work unit. Technical training will need to be developed in regard to data collection and recording details for personnel involved in the forecasting method. This includes production and service personnel who work with customers and production techniques.

Modification of Operational Records

Modification of operational records is needed to some extent in all foodservice organizations. Data recording techniques for the record of customer number, menu item selection, and preference statistics information will need to be documented as discussed in earlier chapters. Many of the production records will need to be modified to reflect the data for the development of databases for foodservice forecasting.

Evaluation Reporting

Evaluation reporting is an important component for the ongoing success of forecasting in foodservice. First of all, the evaluation of the forecasting method as described in Chapter 4 is critical to good forecasting. In addition, an overall operational evaluation is necessary to report back to the controlling personnel such as administrators and owners. The evaluation should include forecasting accuracies, personnel acceptance, cost of maintenance, and results of the other enhancements that have been controlled through the foodservice forecasting. The evaluation reporting over time may include justification for more enhancements such as computer-assisted forecasting and database management.

ANTICIPATED ORGANIZATIONAL GAINS

The major gain in the foodservice as a result of enhanced and controlled forecasting is that of the improved financial "bottom line." Financial gains result from reduced costs of over- and under-produced menu items in the production unit. *Revenue gains* should result with satisfied customers and positive attitudes displayed by the service personnel.

Production and service personnel will be involved in the data input and controlling aspects of the forecasting. They will not be the recipients of extra work created through poor forecasting. Therefore, the work environment and personnel attitude should make the *work areas pleasant.*

Respect is to be gained by controlling personnel due to financial enhancements, operational efficiency, as well as customer and employee satisfaction. In addition to respect, the entire working attitude and customer response will directly relate to outreach *marketability* of the foodservice. The customer and employees will share positive information with friends and community members in regard to the foodservice.

In summary, the forecasting methods as described can be implemented with confidence and expected positive results. The anticipated results are better controlled costs, and positive work environment. The overall impression of the foodservice by controlling personnel will be positive. The customers will report that the foodservice is a dependable place to eat. Employees will share with others that the foodservice is a good place to work. All these attitudes will contribute to the financial "bottom line" success.

WRAP UP

The forecasting methods detailed in this book serve as a guide to foodservice managers and forecasting team members. From these concepts, foodservice managers will be able to discuss with administrators, owners, and other personnel the need for developing and implementing a forecasting method.

The need for a forecasting method by the foodservice manager and other key personnel can be recognized in several ways. The frequency and amount of under- or overproduction is a key indicator in the production unit. Customer satisfaction can be altered when menu item selection is different than anticipated as a result of production error. Profit loss can occur through food cost of substituted menu items and labor costs. An additional indicator of a forecasting need is foodservice personnel attitude changes that could occur as a result of frequent menu changes and under- and over-production problems.

Implementation of a forecasting method has been discussed in the previous chapters. In addition, a conceptual plan, time schedule for development, personnel training, production and service form modification, evaluation reporting, and estimated costs are to be complied for administrators or owner endorsement. The organization will be able to anticipate through a forecasting method a positive contribution to the financial bottom line success as well as positive outreach marketing to community members through satisfied employees and customers.

ACTION

The implementing or "putting it all together" plan for the forecasting method will be dependent on the skills of the foodservice manager. A well-thoughtout foodservice forecasting method needs a well-thoughtout implementation plan. Action areas for such a plan will contain the following:

1. Identify indicators that are present in the foodservice that are a result of an inaccurate forecasting method:

    (a) Under-production or menu items

    (b) Over-production of menu items

    (c) Dissatisfaction of customers

    (d) Profit loss

    (e) Attitude changes in foodservice personnel.

2. Preparing an action plan for acceptance by controlling personnel such as administrators and owners. The action plan will include:

    (a) Conceptual justification and plan

    (b) Personnel training

    (c) Modification of operational records and techniques

    (d) Evaluation reporting.

3. Documenting anticipated organization gains for the controlling personnel.

The foodservice manager will take the leadership to prepare the implementing action plans. The next step in an action plan will be addressed in the following chapter "Computer-Assisted Forecasting."

6

FORECASTING:
COMPUTER-ASSISTED

T he forecasting methods discussed in the previous chapters can be accomplished with the assistance of data processing. Forecasting with computer assistance is as outlined in the Action plan of Chapter 3 except for use of the computer to accumulate and manipulate data. The term manipulate simply means processing the data through the selected forecasting model.

To accomplish computer-assisted forecasting, a program could be written by a programmer to replicate the manual forecasting procedure. However, spreadsheet software readily available from many vendors can be used. Much of the available software is user friendly and provides a framework for both data collection and manipulation.

A spreadsheet is a software program in which columns of numbers are summed. A spreadsheet appears on screen as a matrix of rows and columns in which the intersection is identified as a cell with a unique row and column number or letter. These cells may store or manipulate data according to coded instruction. As shown in Figure 6.1, cells C1 and C2 contain data, cell C3 contains the results of a formula that will manipulate this data. In this example, the formula C1 + C2 = C3 appears in the upper left corner where data entry or editing occurs. This tells you that cell C3 contains the sum of cell 1 and cell 2. That formula could be changed to allow cell 3 to show whatever results you are interested in.

When viewing the spreadsheet, only the result of the formula is seen. When the cursor is positioned at the specific cell, the formula will appear in the command zone at the top left of the screen as shown in Figure 6.1. When the cursor is positioned on a given cell, the entry is made in the command zone. Using spreadsheets to do forecasting is much simpler than programming an individual system since the spreadsheet provides a generic framework for handling the data as opposed to programming for a specific operation.

$$C1 + C2 = C3$$

	A	B	C	D	E	F	G
1			386				
2			350				
3			736				
4							
5							
6							
7							
8							
9							
10							
11							
12							

Figure 6.1 Sample spreadsheet.

CODED INSTRUCTION

As shown in Figures 6.2 and 6.3, customer demand or menu item demand data are entered in cells of the spreadsheet. In Figure 6.2, a spreadsheet is used to illustrate the moving average technique. Customer Demand, column B is summed and divided by 4, the number of observations, the result is the new forecast shown in cell D5. In Figure 6.3, the exponential smoothing technique is used. Customer Demand, column B and Forecast Demand, column C, are multiplied by judgment factor = 0.3, cell C7 is multiplied by 1 − judgment factor = 0.7. The results are summed to give the value in D5. Note formulas are not observable in the spreadsheet but are highlighted in the command zone as shown in Figure 6.2. Information in spreadsheet cells instructs the computer to manipulate data in other cells. Data are entered in some cells while commands to manipulate the data are in other cells. Data can be collected, entered by the data recorded and sorted by the computer, thus simplifying the data collection process. These are features available in most spreadsheet software packages. Rather than having multiple forms, collection can be managed with sorting for like days of the week or menu item. In Figure 6.4, customer demand for Roast Beef served on different days of the week is shown in cells C2 through 7. Customer demand data sorted for Friday are in cells E8 and E9 and for Monday in cells F8 and F9.

Data are entered by the data recorder in a predetermined format. Data can be entered directly or transferred from a word processing package into the spreadsheet. Formulas are entered as determined by the forecaster, who should be familiar with spreadsheet software, to "set up" the spreadsheet for data entry. Basic formulas discussed in Chapter 3 are entered by the data recorder in identified cells to manipulate data for later entry.

Separate spreadsheets can be used to forecast customer count or menu item demand of specific items. Macros,

D5 : @SUM(B4+B5+B6+B7)/4

	A	B	C	D	E	F	G
	Date	Customer Demand		New Forecast			
1	4/8	295					
2	4/15	296					
3	4/22	289					
4	4/29	292					
5	5/6			293			
6							
7							
9							
10							
11							
12							

Figure 6.2 Sample spreadsheet showing forecasting: Moving average, computer-assisted.

	A	B	C	D	E	F	G
1	Date	Customer Demand	Forecast	New Forecast			
2		295	301				
3		296	299				
4		289	298				
5		292	295	294			
6							
7							
8							
9							
10							
11							
12							

Figure 6.3 Sample spreadsheet showing forecasting: Exponential smoothing.

	A	B	C	D	E	F	G
1	Roast Beef		Customer Demand		Friday Customer Demand	Monday Customer Demand	
2	Monday		208				
3	Friday		215				
4	Tuesday		164				
5	Friday		198				
6	Monday		203				
7	Thursday		210				
8					215	208	
9					198	203	
10							
11							
12							

Figure 6.4 Sample spreadsheet showing sorted customer demand data: Computer-assisted.

which are a set of commands grouped into a single command specific to the software can be used to develop automatic systems. Use of macro commands permits data to be entered and processed more quickly to generate forecasts. Manuals accompanying specific software provide instructions for developing macros.

Utilization of automatic systems requires familiarity with spreadsheet software and the forecasting methods described in Chapter 3. The foodservice manager should delegate the implementation of these functions to the data recorder who possesses basic computer skills. The manager or forecasting team makes the forecasting method decisions. The data recorder could then complete the computer implementation functions.

Spreadsheets can be developed to forecast the customer demand with preferences for calculating menu item demand. With this approach, past customer or menu item demand data are collected and forecasting models (formulas) are used to estimate future customer demand. Preferences for individual menu items are then calculated from past data to determine the forecast for each menu item, discussed in Chapter 3. Menu items are labeled 1 and 2 and represent choices for the customer as discussed in Chapter 3. Preference statistics of 0.6 and 0.4 are multiplied by 293, the forecast value in cell B2 as shown in Figure 6.5. An alternative method would be to develop a separate spreadsheet for each menu item to be forecast. The manager may choose to begin the forecasting process with high cost entrees or items prepared in bulk, since these often are over- or underproduced. Short-order items can be managed more easily with manual tabulation than mathematical forecasting methods since food items are produced to serve within a short time span. Eventually all items can be entered into the system if desired.

When using spreadsheet or database software, data, which can be sorted and organized by the computer, are the

	A	B	C	D	E	F
1	New Customer Demand Forecast		Preference Statistic		New Menu Item Forecast	
2	5/6/91	293	Menu item 1 .6	Menu item 2 .4	Menu item 1 176	Menu item 2 117
3						
4						
5						
6						
7						

Figure 6.5 Sample spreadsheet of forecasting with preference statistic, computer-assisted with formula for cell D7 displayed.

	A	B	C	D	E	F	G
1	Date	Customer Demand	Forecast		Absolute Error	Cost[1]	
2		295	301		6	18	
3		296	299		3	9	
4		289	298		9	27	
5		292	295		3	9	
6							
7							
8							
9							
10							
11							
12							

[1]Cost = $3.00 for each error

Figure 6.6 Sample spreadsheet showing error cost calculations.

same as for a manual system. An internal computer calendar, if available, can be used to assign dates, day of week,
and rotation information, thus, reducing the amount of data
to be entered. If a calendar system does not exist in the
computer, this information will need to be entered manually as the data are entered.

Forecast error as discussed in Chapters 2 and 3 can be
calculated by the computer. Formulas for computing errors
are entered into cells of the spreadsheet. Actual and forecast amounts then are compared to generate the error. The
magnitude of the error can be evaluated by using Bias,
MAD, or MSE as discussed in Chapter 4. Forecast error can
be multiplied by an estimated cost for over- or under-
production of the specific menu item. Use of cost information allows the forecaster to see quickly the true results of
forecast error. Figure 6.6 shows the information in spreadsheet cells that result from commands. Column F reflects
the number of errors in column E multiplied by $3.00 for
each error. Costs could include both fixed and variable or
only variable can be included. Fixed costs are those which
do not change with the level of production or volume. Variable costs are those which change with each item produced. Examples of variable costs would be the food and
labor used to produce the individual menu item.

RECIPE ADJUSTMENT

Recipe adjustment, discussed in Chapter 2, also can be
computer-assisted. Spreadsheet or database software can
be used as in the forecasting process. Heading, ingredient,
amount, and procedure information could be entered into
cells for calculation by software commands. Procedures,
discussed in Chapter 2, guide the development of a spreadsheet for recipe adjustment. (See Figures 6.7, 6.8.)

POINT-OF-SALE ENTRY

Data can be entered using either cash register or handheld point-of-sale equipment. Data should be collected from a single entry point, when possible, rather than coded manually or by machine for re-entry. A single entry point refers to computer system(s) designed to enter data when an order is received or cash collected. Decisions about system design should be made before the system is selected, thus preventing re-entering data from order tickets, cash register receipts, or other printed records.

HARDWARE AND SOFTWARE

Software selection precedes hardware (equipment) selection. Basic spreadsheet and database (data storage) software are available for operation on most computer equipment on the market. Generally, equipment already owned will be adequate for forecasting. Although methods discussed in this text require limited data storage, a hard disk will simplify computer-assisted forecasting. The hard disk not only provides more storage capacity, but also facilitates use of the software because insertion and removal of disks is minimized. Backup storage on a temporary device such as a $5\frac{1}{4}''$ or $3\frac{1}{2}''$ disk is recommended so data and system reliability are not threatened by machine or human failure or power outage.

WRAP UP

Computer-assisted forecasting is accomplished easily when approached in a step-by-step manner. Spreadsheet software is recommended since programming for a specific

BLUEBERRY BUCKLE

/ /   -******   -**

EQUIPMENT-MIXER BOWLS - FLAT PADDLES
        12×20×2 INCH PANS-GREASED
        OVEN 350 DEG. F.

RECIPE SOURCE-KSU

02/05/91 12.05 PM   910109


```
    CODE        PERCENT              INGREDIENT
---------------------------------------------------------------
0082093008      27.13      SUGAR GRANULATED

0041002504       9.30      SHORTENING AP
---------------------------------------------------------------
0021020205       8.04      EGGS WHOLE 30 LBS FZN

---------------------------------------------------------------
0082054100       0.58      SALT
0082021252      33.91      FLOUR AP
0031021000       2.33      NON FAT DRY MILK SOLIDS
0082050058       1.26      BAKING POWDER
---------------------------------------------------------------
0000000001      17.44      WATER
```



```
---------------------------------------------------------------
0061000221      21.32      BLUEBERRIES 30 LBS FZN


---------------------------------------------------------------
0082092559       6.98      SUGAR BROWN 50 LBS
0082093008       3.59      SUGAR GRANULATED
0082021252       3.59      FLOUR AP

0082060452       0.10      CINNAMON GROUND

0041000102       2.33      MARGARINE SOLIDS
```

Figure 6.7 Sample spreadsheet showing forecasting: Volume-menu-item.

```
RECIPE CODE - 04-01-4-051-2    STATUS - DEVELOPMENTAL   2
```

```
***NUMBER OF PORTIONS           96
   PORTION SIZE/COST            .156 LBS.   /   $0.0785
   MEAL PATTERN ALLOWANCE       1 OR 2
   SUGGESTED SERVING UTENSIL    SPATULA
   PAN SIZE                     12×20×2 INCH
   NUMBER OF PANS               3
   WEIGHT PER PAN               5.00 LBS.
   HANDLING LOSS                3.00 PERCENT
   MINIMUM BATCH                32 SERVINGS
   MAXIMUM BATCH                544 SERVINGS
   FORECAST UNIT                32
   TOTAL RECIPE WEIGHT/COST     15.4 LBS.   /   $7.5360
   TOTAL RECIPE VOLUME
```

WEIGHTS AND MEASURES	AP/EP	STEP	PROCEDURE
4.2 LBS		A	1. COMBINE IN MIXER BOWL. CREAM ON NO. 2 SPEED
1.4 LBS			10 MINUTES.
1.2 LBS		B	2. ADD. MIX WELL—ABOUT 5 MINUTES.
0.09 LBS		C	3. COMBINE DRY INGREDIENTS
5.2 LBS			IN ANOTHER MIXER BOWL.
0.36 LBS			MIX ON NO. 1 SPEED ONE
0.19 LBS			MINUTE.
2.7 LBS		D	4. ADD ALTERNATELY WITH DRY INGREDIENTS TO CREAMED MIXTURE.
			5. MIX 3 MINUTES ON NO. 1 SPEED. SCRAPE DOWN BOWL.
			6. MIX ON NO. 2 SPEED 10 SECONDS.
			7. SCALE 5.0 LBS PER PAN. SPREAD BATTER EVENLY. MAY BE MIXED AND PANNED THE DAY BEFORE USING. REFRIGERATE UNTIL MORNING THEN FINISH PRODUCT AND BAKE.
3.3 LBS X		E	8. JUST BEFORE BAKING, SPRINKLE 1.0 LBS OVER BATTER IN EACH PAN.
1.1 LBS X		F	9. COMBINE. MIX ON NO. 2 SPEED 5 MINUTES.
0.55 LBS X			
0.55 LBS X			10. SPRINKLE 0.75 LBS OVER EACH PAN.
0.02 LBS X			11. BAKE AT 350 DEG. F. FOR 35-45 MIN.
0.36 LBS X			12. CUT 4 × 8.
			13. ONE PORTION IS ONE SQUARE.

```
LEMON CHICKEN

  / /    -******     -*************************************
```

```
EQUIPMENT-STEAM JACKETED KETTLE
            FRENCH WHIP
            DEEP FAT FRYER



RECIPE SOURCE-KSU 4/88


03/05/90  4.13 PM       900305



    CODE       PERCENT           INGREDIENT
  ------------------------------------------------------------
  0082021058     4.58    CORNSTARCH 100 LBS

  0082093008    12.73    SUGAR GRANULATED
  ------------------------------------------------------------
  0082033005     9.43    VINEGAR CIDER

  0000000001    31.59    WATER
  0063010461    11.32    FZN LEMON JUICE RECONSTITUTED
  ------------------------------------------------------------
  0082061505     0.05    GINGER GROUND


  0082052506     0.09    LEMON PEEL
  0082080208     0.85    SOUP BASE CHICKEN
  0082061408     0.19    GARLIC POWDER
  0082063401     0.05    PEPPER WHITE GROUND
  0082030057     5.66    CATSUP CND
  0041002105     4.72    OIL SALAD 5 GAL
  0082093504    14.15    SYRUP WHITE
  0082032009     4.58    SOY SAUCE
  ------------------------------------------------------------
  0013167707   117.39    CHICKEN NIBBLETS
```

Figure 6.8 Sample spreadsheet showing forecasting: Computer-assisted with error and cost.

```
RECIPE CODE - 16-25-1-085-3     STATUS - DEVELOPMENTAL    2

   ***NUMBER OF PORTIONS         50
      PORTION SIZE/COST          .181 LBS.    /    $0.4386
      MEAL PATTERN ALLOWANCE     ONE PORTION
      SUGGESTED SERVING UTENSIL  SPOON
      PAN SIZE                   12×20×2
      NUMBER OF PANS              1
      WEIGHT PER PAN             8.50 LBS.
      HANDLING LOSS              15.00 PERCENT
      MINIMUM BATCH
      MAXIMUM BATCH
      FORECAST UNIT
      TOTAL RECIPE WEIGHT/COST   10.6 LBS.    /    $21.9300
      TOTAL RECIPE VOLUME
```

WEIGHTS AND MEASURES	AP/EP	STEP	PROCEDURE
0.49 LBS		A	1. COMBINE IN STEAM JACKETED KETTLE.
1.4 LBS			BLEND WITH FRENCH WHIP.
1.0 LBS		B	2. ADD. STIR UNTIL SMOOTH WITH FRENCH WHIP.
3.4 LBS			
1.2 LBS			
1.0 TSP		C	3. ADD. BLEND IN. COOK AND STIR UNTIL MIXTURE IS TRANSLUCENT.
2.9 TSP			
0.09 LBS			
0.02 LBS			
1.0 TSP			
0.60 LBS			
0.50 LBS			
1.5 LBS			
0.49 LBS			
12.5 LBS	X	D	4. DEEP FAT FRY AT 350 DEG.F. FOR 3-4 MINUTES OR UNTIL DONE.
			5. PLACE 5.0 LBS IN 12×20×2 INCH PAN.
			6. POUR 3.5 LBS OF SAUCE OVER CHICKEN. STIR GENTLY TO COAT.
			7. ONE PORTION IS 0.25 LBS OF CHICKEN PLUS 0.181 LBS OF SAUCE (0.431 LBS TOTAL).

operation can seldom be justified. Managers and other forecasting team members may already be familiar with the software and adapt very quickly.

For those who are unfamiliar, understanding the forecasting methods and basic software capabilities are requisite to successful computer-assisted forecasting. This book should provide adequate information for forecasting. Manuals and tutorial packages included with most software will quickly prepare the forecaster for proper use of the software (spreadsheet) selected. Hardware should be selected to accommodate the desired software. Since the types of software discussed in this book are readily available for most hardware, compatible basic spreadsheet software must be selected.

ACTION

As with a manual system, the forecasting team will select the forecast method. The action follows:

1. Become familiar with mathematical forecasting models described in earlier chapters of this book.
2. Select the forecasting model to be used.
3. Review data source documents and locate forecasting data.
4. Identify single entry point for data, for example, the first point at which usable data can be collected and stored for use throughout the entire forecasting and production process.
5. Develop database using appropriate software by entering data into appropriate cells of the spreadsheet.
6. Enter commands required by software to manipulate data to produce forecast. For example, some

cells will contain the formulas specified to calculate the forecast using the data stored in other cells.

7. Enter commands to monitor the forecast method whether tabular or graphic as discussed in Chapter 4. Forecast error can be calculated and costed, when appropriate, by computer.

Appendix A

RECIPE ADJUSTMENT

INCREASING OR DECREASING RECIPE YIELDS

Changing yields for recipes may be required to meet the needs of individual situations. Recipes may need to be adjusted to produce batch sizes compatible with preparation equipment, such as mixers, ovens, and steam-jacketed kettles, or consistent with pan sizes available. Recipes may also need adjustment as portion sizes are increased or decreased or as purchase units for ingredients change.

Three methods commonly used to adjust recipe yields are the *factor method,* the *percentage method,* and *direct-reading measurement tables.*

Factor Method*

In the factor method, a conversion factor is determined and multiplied by each ingredient in the recipe. This process is explained in the following steps:

Step 1 Divide the desired yield by the known yield of the recipe being adjusted to obtain the

---

* Shugart, G., and Molt, M., *Food for Fifty,* 8th ed. (New York: Macmillan, 1989) pp. 53–56.

conversion *factor*. For example, to increase a 50-portion recipe to 125 portions, divide 125 by 50 for a factor of 2.5.

Step 2 Wherever possible, convert ingredients to weight. If amounts of some ingredients are too small to be weighed, leave then in measure.

Step 3 Multiply the amount of each ingredient in the original recipe by the factor.

Step 4 Multiply the original total weight of ingredients by the factor. Multiply the pounds and ounces separately.

Step 5 Add together the new weights of all ingredients for the adjusted recipe. If the answers in Steps 4 and 5 are not the same, an error exists and the calculations should be checked. (A slight difference may exist because of rounding the figures.)

Step 6 Change weights of any ingredients that can be more easily measured than weighed to measure.

See Table A.1 for an example.

Percentage Method

The percentage method of recipe adjustment often is desirable, especially for large-volume production where batch sizes may vary greatly. Once the ingredient percentage has been established, it remains constant for all future adjustments. Recipe increases or decreases are made by multiplying the percentage of each ingredient by the total weight desired. Checking ingredients for proper recipe balance is possible, because the percentage of each ingredient is available. Some computer recipe systems use the percentage

Figure A.1 The Following Example Illustrates the Procedure for Adjusting the Baking Powder Biscuits Recipe from 100 Biscuits to 500, Using the Factor Method of Adjustment:

Step 1 Derive the factor: $\dfrac{500 \text{ (new)}}{100 \text{ (original)}} = 5$ (factor)

Ingredients	Original Recipe	Step 2 Convert to Weight	Step 3 Multiply by Factor	Steps 6 and 7 Change to Measure and Simplify
Flour, all-purpose	5 lb	5 lb	25 lb	25 lb
Baking powder	5 oz	5 oz	25 oz	1 lb 9 oz
Salt	2 Tbsp	1⅓ oz	6½ oz	6½ oz
Shortening, hydrogenated	1 lb 4 oz	1 lb 4 oz	6 lb 4 oz	6 lb 4 oz
Milk	1¾ qt	3 lb 8 oz	17 lb 8 oz	2 gal + ¾ qt
Steps 4 and 5				
Total weight		10 lb 2 oz	50 lb 11 oz	

Source: Reprinted by permission of Macmillan Publishing Company from *Food for Fifty* 8th ed. by G. Shugart, and M. Molt. Copyright © 1989 by Macmillan Publishing Company.

123

method of recipe adjustment. This process is explained in the following steps:

Step 1 Convert all ingredients from measure or pounds and ounces to pounds and tenths of a pound. Make desired equivalent ingredient substitutions such as frozen whole eggs for fresh eggs, nonfat dry milk and water for liquid milk. Use edible portion (EP) weights when a difference exists between EP and as purchased (AP) weights. Individual meat items and other meats in entree recipes that do not require the meat to be cooked prior to combining with other ingredients are calculated on AP weight. Examples are pork chops, meat loaf, and Salisbury steak.

Step 2 Total the weight of ingredients in the recipe, using EP weight where applicable.

Step 3 Calculate the percentage of each ingredient in relation to the total weight, using the following formula:

$$\frac{\text{Individual Ingredient Weight}}{\text{Total Weight}} = \frac{\text{Percentage of}}{\text{Each Ingredient}}$$

The sum of the percentages must equal 100.

Step 4 Check the ratio of ingredients. Standards have been established for ingredient proportions of many items. The ingredients should be in proper balance before going further.

Step 5 Establish the weight needed to give the desired number of servings. The weight will be determined by portion size multiplied by the desired number of servings to be prepared. This weight may need to be adjusted because of pan sizes or equipment capacity.

Step 6 Handling loss must be added to the weight needed, and it may vary from 1 to 10 percent, depending on the product. Similar items produce predictable losses, and with some experimentation these losses can be assigned accurately. The formula for incorporating handling loss is as follows:

$$\frac{\text{Total}}{\text{Weight Needed}} = \frac{\text{Desired Yield}}{\frac{100}{\text{Percent}} - \frac{\text{Assigned Handling}}{\text{Loss Percent}}}$$

For example, cake has a handling loss of approximately 2 percent, and 72 lb of batter is needed to make nine $18 \times 26 \times 2$-inch pans. To determine the total amount of batter to be made, divide 72 lb by 98 percent (100 percent − 2 percent handling loss). Using this formula, a recipe calculated for 73.47 lb of batter is needed.

Step 7 Multiply each ingredient percentage by the total weight to give the exact amount of each ingredient needed. The total weight of ingredients should equal the weight needed as calculated in Step 6. Once the percentages of a recipe have been established, any number of servings can be calculated, and the ratio of ingredients to the total will remain the same.

Step 8 Unless scales are calibrated to read in pounds and tenths of a pound, convert to pounds and ounces or to measure.

See Table A.2 for an example.

Figure Appendix A.2 The Following Example Illustrates the Procedure for Adjusting the Baking Powder Biscuit Recipe from 100 Biscuits to 500, Using the Percentage Method of Adjustment.

Ingredients	Original Recipe	Step 1 Convert to Decimal Weights	Step 3 Calculate Percentage	Step 7 Calculate Weights	Step 8 Convert to Pounds and Ounces
Flour, all-purpose	5 lb	5.0 lb	49.276	25.52 lb	25 lb 8 oz
Baking powder	5 oz	0.313 lb	3.085	1.60 lb	1 lb 10 oz
Salt	2 Tbsp	0.0839 lb	0.827	0.43 lb	6¾ oz
Shortening, hydrogenated	1 lb 4 oz	1.25 lb	12.319	6.38 lb	6 lb 6 oz
Milk	1¾ qt	3.5 lb	34.493	17.86 lb	2¼ gal
Step 2 Total Weight		10.1469 lb	100.00	51.79 lb	

Step 4 Check ratio of ingredients to see if they are within acceptable guidelines.

Step 5 Establish needed weight:

$$\frac{10.1469 \text{ (Total Weight of 100 Biscuits)}}{100} = 0.1015 \text{ lb (Weight per Biscuit)}$$

500 (Desired Yield) × 0.1015 lb = 50.75 lb Dough Needed before Handling Loss

Step 6 Calculate handling loss. Estimated handling loss equals 2 percent:

$$\frac{50.75 \text{ lb (Desired Yield)}}{98 \text{ Percent}} = 51.79 \text{ lb Total Dough Needed}$$

Source: Reprinted by permission of Macmillan Publishing Company from *Food for Fifty* 8th ed. by G. Shugart and M. Molt. Copyright © 1989 by Macmillan Publishing Company.

Appendix B

SUPPLEMENT CASES

CHAPTER 1

A. A foodservice manager in a family dining unit believes that the supervisor who orders food does not use many past records to forecast. The records "mean nothing" as many of the customers order ½ servings of the entrees and that "fouls up the count."

Discussion Questions

1. How could the ½ serving be tabulated?
2. Comments about the foodservice are collected in a customer suggestion box and many customers state that they are disappointed when "food runs out" and they have to choose something else. What would be a solution?
3. What records could be used in the family dining unit to show customer count?
4. How could the manager begin to develop a forecasting method?

B. A hospital patient foodservice manager is concerned about the lack of freezer space for purchased and prepared food items. The cooks complain that there is no room to store leftover menu items. When checking the purchasing amounts of foods, the manager realizes that there has not been any changes over the past year. The manager proceeds to plan to order an additional freezer so that the cooks will not complain.

Discussion Questions

1. What record keeping methods could be suggested for freezer control?
2. Could the lack of space in the freezer be related to forecasting?
3. Who should monitor the management of the freezer?
4. What solutions other than purchasing a freezer could the manager consider?

CHAPTER 2

A. A foodservice has two serving units and data are being collected to determine the pattern of customers census. Monday through Sunday data from unit 1 is 175, 212, 225, 222, 173, 100, 97 for week 1 and 166, 190, 193, 200, 158, 113, 117 for week 2. Data from unit 2 is 112, 120, 119, 124, 127, 119, 123 for week 1 and 130, 150, 100, 160, 158, 165, 163 for week 2.

Discussion Questions

1. What data census pattern and type of foodservice unit are represented in unit one?

2. What data census pattern is represented in unit two? Discuss the action that management could take in estimating future forecasts for unit 2.

3. How much data would you recommend should be collected from units one and two to assure confidence that these data represent the units.

4. How should the cooks respond to the customer census data?

B. A college residence hall foodservice director states that forecasting is impossible and cannot be considered for the residence hall foodservice. The director believes that the strength of the foodservice is the policy of "second" and "third" servings for each student. The director is concerned that forecasting would restrict the number of servings to one per person.

Discussion Questions

1. How could the customer census be used to estimate the amount of food to produce?

2. Would the number of servings per customer need to be changed?

3. What would be the best measure to use in menu item forecasting, such as portions, number of plates used, or number of counter pans?

4. Would forecasting restrict the amount of food served to each person?

C. The cooks of a hospital foodservice have difficulty planning the amount of menu items to prepare for the selective menu. The patients served last often have substituted menu items and patient complaints are numerous. The tally of number of portions for noon and night meals is recorded by 10:30 A.M. each day for the cooks to follow. Breakfast "tally" is rarely used as the cooks can quickly provide additional food or substitutions if there is a shortage. Noon and night menu item records are a problem with admission and discharge of patients throughout the day.

Discussion Questions

1. How can accurate menu item counts be collected to build a database?

2. Who would be responsible for developing an accurate database?

3. What training would need to occur to foodservice personnel in regard to menu item data collection? Who would need to receive the training?

4. How often would menu item data need to be collected?

5. How can menu item data be used in the forecasting method? In what manner should it be arranged?

CHAPTER 3

A. In the organization of a forecasting team, the topics most discussed were: (1) Who will take leadership in the organization of the forecasting method? and (2) How can a forecasting method be developed and implemented in the ongoing operation?

Discussion Questions

1. Who would be the person *most likely* to be interested in learning the forecasting formulas?
2. How could the forecasting model formulas be used in a everyday procedure in a foodservice?
3. Could the formulas be included on a production worksheet? Discuss the possibilities.
4. How could the forecasting method be presented to foodservice employees so that they would take the procedure seriously? What would be the employees' responsibilities?

B. The forecasting methods, moving average and simple exponential smoothing, are recommended for use in most foodservice organizations. However, the supervisor in a cafeteria foodservice has been employed for 25 years and won't listen to any discussion about forecasting models. The supervisor's forecasting method is subjective and works well as the cafeteria never runs out of food. Actually, plenty of "leftovers" are always available to serve as substitutions when food runs out because of additional customers. Substitutions are okay because customers probably would not know what was on the original menu if the menu board was changed.

Discussion Questions

1. Discuss the pros and cons of the supervisor's forecasting method.
2. How would a manager begin to obtain census and menu item demand data?
3. How would the manager encourage the supervisor to think about forecasting?
4. How could the use of forecasting models be introduced to the supervisor?
5. Plan the steps needed to gain the supervisor's interest in reviewing data, learning forecasting and becoming a member of the forecasting team?

C. An administrator or controlling officer has been introduced to the final stages of the forecasting method. In the process of updating this administrator, the simple exponential forecasting model has been described. The administrator claims to be interested but, in an authority position states that the foodservice should always use a judgment value of 0.9 because "we always use the biggest and the best in this organization."

Discussion Questions

1. Should the forecaster use a judgment value 0.9 in the forecasting model as the officer demanded? Discuss.
2. What action should be taken to train the officer?
3. What effect would a judgment value 0.9 have on the foodservice?
4. How could the operating cost be affected with a judgment value 0.9 as a constant value?

CHAPTER 4

A. A hospital foodservice manager has implemented forecasting in both the employee cafeteria and the patient meal service. A specific forecast method was chosen by the manager but evaluation of the forecast error was not done. The forecast team stated that the forecasting method would not be changed once it was put into place.

Discussion Questions

1. Should the manager evaluate the method?
2. How could the evaluation be implemented?
3. How often would an evaluation need to be done?
4. Would evaluation change the costs of the foodservice? How? Discuss various evaluation techniques as they relate to daily operations.

B. Forecasting confidence needs to be a strength and result of a good forecasting method. Forecasting team members should be able to rely on the results and to share their confidence with production and service foodservice personnel.

Discussion Questions

1. What steps in the forecasting method would help assure confidence?
2. Do the members of the forecasting team need to check the forecasting model daily?
3. How can the forecasting method affect the food and labor budget?
4. What methods could be used to assist the forecasting team in building their forecasting model? How

could these methods be explained to the corporate controlling officer?

C. A forecast error is the only error data that is understood by the head cook. The cook will not listen or support the idea of forecast error or acknowledge forecasting formulas. The other production employees are not wanting to be involved with the idea or process of this new forecasting method.

Discussion Questions

1. Does the head cook need to understand forecasting error measurements and forecasting models?
2. Can forecast error be used when the error measurements of Bias, MAD, or MSE are not used?
3. Where is the forecast error recorded?
4. How is the forecast error different then a list of leftover foods?
5. What training would be necessary for the foodservice production personnel to understand the forecast error?

CHAPTER 6

A. A director of a foodservice suggests that a computer could be used for forecasting. The forecasting team has no member who knows how to type and, therefore, will not listen to ideas about using a computer. The manager, head cook, and data recorder have all been employed for ten or more years and consider themselves too old to learn new techniques.

Discussion Questions

1. What should the director do in regard to:
   a. Personnel?
   b. Computer?
   c. Forecasting method?
2. Is typing an important skill for the forecasting team members?

B. The forecasting team is interested in using a computer to assist them in forecasting. Currently, the computer is used by an office assistant only for correspondence.

Discussion Questions

1. How could forecasting be integrated into the computer process?
2. What would be the benefit of hiring someone, from an office pool of employees who use the computer, to do the forecasting?
3. What would be the simplest data to collect before training someone to use the computer?

C. A computer and printer with software were purchased by the previous foodservice manager. He/She is no longer iwth the company and the computer is "collecting dust." As manager, you know how to turn the machine on but that is all. Some of the high school and college students who work for you are somewhat computer literate bu tare "too busy" to help you. You know you need to improve forecasting in your operation.

Discussion Questions

1. Where do you begin?
2. Is forecasting with computer-assistance important enough to alter the system to accommodate?
3. Are there ways management and employee time could be adjusted to allow those who are computer literate or interested to develop and maintain systems?
4. Should someone be hired to develop and implement system?

Glossary of Terms

Bias: An error measurement technique in which the sum of forecast errors is divided by the total number of observations. It shows any tendency to over- and under-forecast.

Bottom Line: Business term to identify the financial status of the organization, such as profit or loss dollar amount.

Break Even: Financial position in which volume of business produces sales or income equal to expenditures.

Cells: Spaces in a spreadsheet for storing data or formula.

Census: Total number of customers for a meal. Function of current customer census or count.

Control Chart: Graphic presentation used to make decisions about the data or control of the production system.

Covers: Each customer's place setting for a meal, including linens, paper, flatware, glassware, and dinnerware.

Customer: Person or persons purchasing food or service. These customers include people identified as a customer, client, patient, resident, or staff.

Customer Demand: Customer count or census.

Data: Factual information used as a basis or reasoning, discussion, or calculations.

Database: A file of information that is stored in a manual or computer file.

Data Recorder: Person who is responsible for the food production records.

Electronic Data Processing: Manipulation of data according to specific commands using electronic equipment, i.e. computers.

Food Item: Purchased or inventory food, pre-production or served food.

Food Production Operation: All activities in a restaurant or other foodservice that relate to the production of food, such as food, equipment, personnel, documents, and space.

Foodservice Manager: Person who has the responsibility for the management of the entire food production operation.

Forecast: Technique to utilize past information/data in a systematic way to estimate future needs.

Forecast Amount: Amount of food estimated to prepare (servings or weight) for the forecast date.

Forecast Error: Difference of the forecast amount and the customer demand.

Forecaster: Person who is trained to generate or forecast the volume of menu items needed in the future.

Forecasting Models: Mathematical expression of estimated future events.

Hardware: Equipment used to process data, the tangible computer components.

Head Cook: Technically skilled person responsible for preparing the menu items.

Judgment Factor: A coefficient, Alpha, between 0 and 1 used to smooth the randomness of data.

Lead Time: Time that elapses between the time the forecast is generated and time it is used.

Macro Commands: Sets of commands to perform broader functions at greater speed.

Manipulation: Use of data to generate outcomes according to program instructions.

Mean Absolute Deviation: An error measurement in which the sum of the absolute forecast errors are divided by the total number of observations. It provides an average of forecast errors without a sign (−) or (+).

Mean Squared Error: An error measurement in which the sum of the squared forecast errors are divided by the total observations. It provides a value that penalizes a forecast with extreme or large errors.

Menu: Planned list of items from which the customer may select a meal.

Menu Category: Function of a menu item, for example, appetizer, entree, dessert.

Menu Cycle: A group of menus that are repeated within a time period.

Menu Item: Each food or recipe item offered per menu meal.

Moving Average Model: Average of customer demand for a specified number of times; the most recent demand data are added and the oldest is dropped to keep the data current.

Order: Amount of food to purchase in order to produce the menu items.

Point of Sale: Point at which sale transaction occurs.

Prediction: Subjective, intuitive technique to estimate a future event, not necessarily with the use of past data.

Preference Statistic: Proportion or percentage of customers making a choice.

Production Unit: Kitchen or back of the house areas.

Profit: Additional dollars shown after the expenses of food, labor, supplies, and overhead have been paid from the sales income.

Quantitative: A measurement in terms of quantity or amounts.

Restaurant Menu: A set menu (a one-day menu) offering several choices in each menu category.

Simple Exponential Smoothing Model: An averaging method that uses both the customer demand and the forecast value for the same day and includes a judgment value.

Single Entry Point of Data: Entry of data at time of order for use throughout the system.

Smoothing: A process to estimate numerical values minimizing random values that are atypical from the data.

Software: Commands used to manipulate data for desired outcomes.

Sorted: Data are arranged according to the same menu item, day of the week or meal.

Source Documents: The record that contains the data. This record will always serve as the source of the data, such as point of sale report has the record of the number of each menu item sold per meal and day.

Spreadsheet: Array of rows and columns in which data can be stored and processed.

Time-Series Model: Model which is based on the assumption that actual occurrences follow an identifiable trend over time.

Tolerance Limits: Upper and lower bounds of acceptable error values recorded on a control chart.

Index

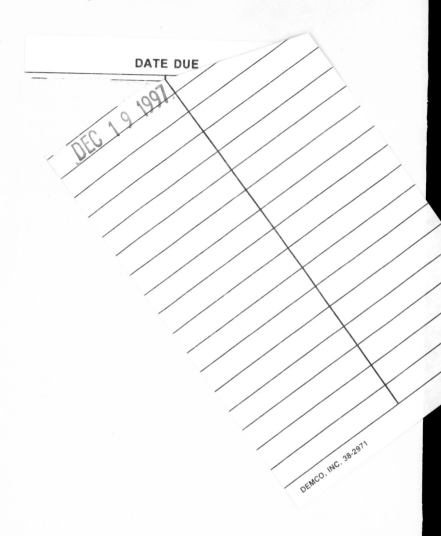